CW01521911

Cleto SAPORETTI

Cleto SAPORETTI

The remarkable life of a
prisoner of war,
poultry farmer, and
health-promoting philanthropist

Geraldine Mitton

Quickfox
publishing

Published by Quickfox Publishing
PO Box 12028 Mill Street 8010
Cape Town, South Africa
www.quickfox.co.za
info@quickfox.co.za
Tel: 0861 234 256 | Fax: 0865 600 444

First published 2013

CLETO SAPORETTI
ISBN 978-0-620-55947-8

Copyright © Geraldine Mitton

All rights reserved. No part of this publication may be reproduced,
stored in a retrieval system, or transmitted, in any form or by any means,
without the prior written permission of the publisher.

Editor – Georgina Hatch
Cover and book designer – Vanessa Wilson
Typesetting and production – Quickfox Publishing
Printing – MegaDigital, Cape Town

ACKNOWLEDGEMENTS

Although I did not know Cleto personally, my own life story has been interwoven with Saporetti-related events which occurred in the 1960s and throughout subsequent years, leading to my leaving academic medicine in 1986. It was a great privilege and an exciting journey to have the opportunity to translate his vision into reality.

I was assisted by dietician Cornelia Kirsten who evaluated new research emerging in the field of nutrition. Working side by side we were like explorers. In the 80s there were many "nutritional flat earthers". Cornelia also supervised the work of our nutrition educators. Professor Leonie van Heerden encouraged us to promote vegetable gardening in the community, decades before it was introduced elsewhere.

Executor of the Saporetti estate, Graeme Dale Kuys, was totally supportive of the aims of the Saporetti Foundation until his death in 1992.

Many, if not most, of Cleto's friends and associates have passed on, but I was able to obtain many stories and anecdotes from their families.

I would like to thank Dr Emilio Coccia from Zonderwater, and the South African Military History Society for information about Zonderwater, which seemed to be more of a happy Italian village than a grim WW2 prison.

The Classense Library in Ravenna supplied photographs of soldiers in WW1.

Leonardo Senni found photographs of Cleto as a young man in his mother's collection.

Allan Stuart, son of Alistair Stuart who employed Cleto as a parolee, and Dirk Serdyn current owner of Lemoenkloof, gave information about early days in the poultry industry.

Willy de Villiers was able to recall, in detail, the rise and fall of Lemoenkloof and its renaissance as Lemoenkloof Holdings where he was MD.

Thanks go to Renata Vernetti for assisting with Italian translations, also to Maria Fiorovanti and Maria Grazia Martinengo. Theresa du Plessis and Ron Hobkirk were involved in the early days at the Hydro; later Graham Hunter and Juan van Breda gave helpful information. Judy Ayre recalled her times with Aunt Letty Godfrey.

Leon and Tony Chaitow, as well as Brian Wilson, provided information about Dr Boris Chaitow.

Emiliano Sandri, Giuseppe Caputo, Paulina Chisin, Michelina Ciman, Ernesto Partisani and Orlando Valacchi all contributed stories and memories.

Lastly, my thanks go to Georgina Hatch and Vanessa Wilson for their expert editing and layout of this book.

Geraldine Mitton
Cape Town, 2013

FOREWORD I

EDOARDO VITALI, *Consul of Italy in Cape Town, 2012*

The relationship of Italians with South Africa is an impassioned affair. Many interesting publications are available but, most probably, there is much more to say. The presence of Italians in this country goes back many centuries but seems to develop more prominently during periodic moments of intense migration. Due to the Unification of Italy in 1861, the end of the 19th century saw many a skilled farmer, artisan and labourer leave for pastures new. The end of WWII again saw many persons seek a better future out of their national border and in many cases, they succeeded in improving their lives.

The trend continues to this day; many young Italian professionals and small business entrepreneurs are coming to South Africa as the economic crisis has hit Europe apparently far more than elsewhere. Through the ages, Italians and persons of Italian origin have left a bold and durable imprint, at times controversial, but mostly their pursuit of excellence is recognised. They are loved and criticised worldwide with unconditional intensity according to a sensationalised stereotype. Their footprint is never commonplace and never ordinary. Stonemasons and engineers, doctors and lawyers, wine makers, restaurateurs, tailors and businessmen: in a thousand different ways, Italians who have made the world their country have diffused and transmitted their 'Italianity'. An Italian way that is visible to this day even in the streets of Cape Town and South Africa through restaurants, boutiques, and in the names of streets, squares and towns.

It is therefore tenable that the adventures and, in a certain way romantic, events of Cleto Saporetti's life are no exception to the rule. His story relates to the story of many men of the past century who found themselves in an era of dramatic events. Their courage, intelligence and perseverance not only allowed them to overcome great difficulties, but gave them the ability to seize opportunities that led to unimaginable successes.

Born in Ravenna in 1905, at the time when Italy was not even 50 years old and the world was still divided between independent states and colonies, Saporetti became an entrepreneur and made his way to Ethiopia to seek his fortune. WWll and his enlistment changed his destiny. He was captured and arrived in South Africa as a prisoner of war and decided to stay after the end of hostilities. After many ups and downs he acquired a poultry farm that he ran very successfully. Again his destiny mutated as a flu epidemic made his successful business totally inconsequential. At the age of 53 he had to change course and start from scratch. He then embarked on a voyage in a totally different direction and started a wellness centre offering natural therapeutic treatments, for which he is still remembered today.

This extraordinary man's success was recognised already in 1969 and he was awarded a knighthood, namely Commendatura dell'Ordine al Merito della Repubblica Italiana. After his death, a foundation bearing his name was formed. His social and professional life is a testament to the courage that is often required to overcome the challenges of life. He did not only contribute metaphorically to life's challenges but, with hard work, he gave of himself for the benefit of all in his adopted country without ever forgetting the land of his birth. The book that follows is a fitting tribute to Cleto Saporetti and ensures that his memory is transmitted also through his Foundation. It will be of great interest for many who, like myself, would never have been afforded the opportunity of meeting him by reason of date of birth.

Translated by Maria Grazia Martinengo (Cav)
Cape Town, 3 December 2012

PREFAZIONE I

EDOARDO VITALI, *Console d'Italia, Cape Town 2012*

Quella degli Italiani in Sud Africa è una vicenda appassionante. Su di essa sono state scritte molte interessanti pubblicazioni ma molto, probabilmente, resta ancora da dire. La presenza italiana in questo Paese va indietro a lungo nel tempo e sembra svilupparsi intorno a periodici, intensi movimenti migratori. Alla fine del diciannovesimo secolo, come parte della massiccia emigrazione successiva all'Unità di Italia che portò, nei più diversi angoli di mondo, agricoltori qualificati e sapienti artigiani ed operai. Al termine della seconda guerra mondiale, quando molti cercarono e, in moltissimi casi, trovarono fuori dai confini nazionali l'opportunità per un futuro migliore.

Anche al giorno d'oggi arrivano in Sud Africa molti Italiani, spesso giovani professionisti o piccoli imprenditori, in fuga dalla crisi economica che in Europa stacolpendo apparentemente più duro che altrove. Attraverso i decenni, la comunità italiana o di origine italiana ha saputo imprimere al Paese che l'ha ospitata un'impronta decisa, durevole; a volte controversa ma quasi sempre votata all'eccellenza, secondo stereotipi estremizzati che, nel mondo, portano gli Italiani ad essere amati o criticati con la stessa incondizionata intensità. Di certo, un'impronta mai banale ed ordinaria. Scalpellini ed ingegneri, medici ed avvocati; viticoltori, ristoratori, sarti e uomini di affari: in mille diversi modi gli Italiani che hanno fatto del mondo il loro Paese hanno saputo diffondere e trasmettere l'essenza della propria italianità. Un'italianità che è presente e visibile ancora oggi, anche per le strade di Cape Town e del Sud Africa, nelle insegne di ristoranti e di boutique, nei nomi di grandi aziende e di studi legali, nella toponomastica di strade, piazze e città.

In questo senso, la vicenda avventurosa ed in certo modo romantica di Cleto Saporetti non fa eccezione. La sua storia è comune a quella di molti altri uomini del secolo passato che, trovatisi a vivere in un'epoca di eventi drammatici e grandi, seppero affrontare con coraggio, intelligenza e perseveranza le sfide dei tempi, cogliendo le opportunità in esse dischiuse e raggiungendo successi inizialmente inimmaginabili. Nato a Ravenna nel 1905, quando l'Italia unita non aveva neanche 50 anni, Saporetti si fece imprenditore e cercò fortuna in Etiopia, in un mondo ancora diviso tra Stati liberi e colonie. La seconda guerra mondiale e l'arruolamento cambiarono il suo destino, facendolo arrivare, come prigioniero di guerra, in Sud Africa. Paese nel quale decise ed ottenne, al termine del conflitto, di rimanere. In maniera un po' rocambolesca Saporetti acquisì un'azienda di allevamento, che condusse con successo, fin quando il destino mutò ancora una volta il corso della sua vita. Un'epidemia aviaria azzerò le sue fortune e lo costrinse, all'età di 53 anni, a ripartire da zero. Questa volta dedicò le sue energie all'apertura di un centro benessere basato sulla applicazione di terapie naturali, attività alla quale rimane ancora oggi principalmente legata la sua memoria.

La cifra straordinaria dell'esperienza di Saporetti, che proseguì anche dopo la sua morte con la fondazione che ne prese il nome, ha trovato riconoscimento con la concessione, già nel 1969, della Commendatura dell'Ordine al Merito della Repubblica Italiana. La sua vicenda umana e professionale resta ancora di esempio per chiaffronta con coraggio e spesso vince le sfide della vita; per chi nel viaggio non solo metaforico dell'esistenza contribuisce, con l'attività del proprio lavoro, al benessere ed al progresso della terra che lo ospita, senza per questo dimenticare i legami con la terra che l'ha visto nascere. Il libro che segue rende giusto omaggio alla memoria di Cleto Saporetti e vuole far tesoro, attraverso il racconto della sua vicenda biografica, del suo lascito. Che, sono sicuro, sarà di interesse e di stimolo anche per chi, come me, per ragioni anagrafiche non avrebbe mai potuto conoscerlo.

FOREWORD II

ALLAN STUART, *Dundarach Poultry Farm, Western Cape, October 2012*

My father, Alastair Stuart, had shortly before the onset of the war employed Bob James as his poultry manager. James had come to South Africa from Britain with all the latest poultry farming techniques and had established a reputation in South Africa for up-to-date poultry husbandry. During the war my father had been allocated ten Italian POWs whom he set to work on building our first intensive breeding and brooding houses. Many of these buildings still stand. In terms of the Geneva Convention these men had to be repatriated at the end of the war, so this left a great gap in the farm's workforce.

As my father had been very satisfied with the workmanship and work ethic of the Italians, he decided to sign permanent employment contracts and immigration papers for two Italians, Farinella, who was to run the hatchery, and Cleto Saporetti – or Sapo, as we knew him – to run the anthracite brooders. My dad built a two-bedroomed house for Mr Farinella and his wife, and a single room for Sapo, who was unmarried. This single room still stands and is currently used as a farm store.

However, Sapo was too able and too ambitious to continue at Dundarach, and at the end of his year's contract he decided to go it alone. In the year that he was with us he bought an old motor bike and visited various people in the neighbourhood, including Ben Godfrey. Ben owned and lived on a neighbouring farm, Lemoenkloof, which was just over the Paardeberg from Dundarach. Ben owned a lime factory at Moorresberg and used Lemoenkloof merely as his residence and did not farm it commercially due to lack of permanent water supply. As this book relates, Sapo made a deal with Godfrey and used the poultry husbandry experience that he had gained at Dundarach to build up a poultry empire.

Thereafter our family kept in regular contact with Sapo. During my nine years at boarding school I watched in awe as Sapo's business rose and eventually surpassed by far our own poultry business at Dundarach. As I grew older and took over my father's business I had many discussions with Sapo in which he shared with me the core secrets of his success. I consider Sapo to be one of my mentors.

Sapo, like many Italians, had this wonderful convivial way with his customers, both restauranteurs and shop keepers. In those days there were no impersonal chain stores with central distribution depots. Each customer, each sale, required a person-to-person relationship at which Sapo excelled. In addition to the farm at Lemoenkloof, Sapo built a smart distribution cool room and depot at Paarden Eiland. At his peak, before Newcastle Disease struck, he had 26 trucks delivering to his numerous customers.

Sapo's success in the 1950s and 1960s was based on his belief in "vertical integration". On the farming site of Lemoenkloof he had breeders, layers, broilers, a hatchery, an abbatoir, an egg-packing station and a feed mill. He believed that the secret of success was to take multiple margins on the multiple links in the production chain.

Added to Lemoenkloof was his distribution and delivery system in Paarden Eiland and he had the whole operation, from the bags of grain, vertically integrated.

Having all these operations, with multiple ages of poultry on one site, worked well when the country was reasonably disease free. However, new diseases such as P.P.L.O. (pleuro-pneumonia like organisms), infectious bronchitis, infectious laryngo-tracheitis, and eventually Newcastle Disease, started spreading to South Africa from imported breeding stock, and from live poultry kept on board the numerous ships that passed by Cape Town when the Suez Canal was closed. These diseases became progressively more difficult to control, and Bob James banned us school boys from visiting Lemoenkloof for fear of carrying the new diseases back to Dundarach. Ultimately, Newcastle disease resulted in the State Vet closing Lemoenkloof down, slaughtering all the poultry and burying them in trenches.

For some time Sapo was despondent, but eventually agreed to a management buyout by his manager, Willie de Villiers, and others, with the formation of Lemoenkloof Holdings.

Sapo's belief in vertical integration was a clear step forward from Bob James's belief in the single link production of day-old chicks. However, a new generation of British immigrants – Trevor Tincker of Rainbow, Ken Spiller of Festive, and Jack Warrener of Harvest Chickens – had already started to take the broiler industry another step forward through "horizontal integration" and minimizing cross infection of the younger chicks from older hens. This is not to say that Sapo's concept of vertical integration had failed; many of the horizontally-integrated broiler operations, in turn, became vertically integrated when they were bought by feed millers or when they, themselves, built their own mills – thus vindicating Sapo's concept.

Even before the Newcastle Disease debacle, Sapo's interest had moved from poultry to human health. When visiting him at Lemoenkloof, one would be offered a carrot juice instead of tea or coffee. Sapo kept in contact with his past friends and invited my mother around to Blijdskap which had an old Cape Dutch farmhouse where Sapo spent the occasional weekend. Sapo had been forced to buy Blijdskap, which adjoined Lemoenkloof, in order to get a dam site and secure water for his poultry.

Later, he invited me to see his High Rustenberg Hydro. I was interested in his social responsibility philosophy which included providing each member of his staff with a house on the estate, or in Stellenbosch.

His legacy to me is a long and lasting respect for the Italian community in South Africa, the importance of personal contact and rapport with one's customers, a social responsibility to one's staff, and the concept of vertical integration in poultry production.

Allan Stuart
Dundarach Poultry Farm
Western Cape Province

TABLE OF CONTENTS

CHRONOLOGY

CLETO SAPORETTI 1905–1984

1905............... Cleto Saporetti is born in Ravenna, Italy. Saporetti family moves to Cocciolia during World War 1

1930............... Cleto works as a road engineer in Ravenna

1937............... Cleto works as a road engineer in Ethiopia and Eritrea

1940............... Cleto is conscripted into *Camicie Nere* (Black Shirts); Italy enters World War 2

1941............... Cleto is captured by British forces in Massawa, Eritrea; transported by ship to Durban in South Africa

1941–1946... Prisoner of War No. 258419, Zonderwater Prison, Pretoria

1947............... Released on parole to Dundarach Farm, Klipheuwel in the Western Cape, owned by Alistair Stewart

1948............... Moves to Lemoenkloof Poultry Farm, Klipheuwel; works for owner Ben Godfrey

1950............... Purchases Lemoenkloof with nine post-dated cheques

1954............... Marries Ben Godfrey's sister Letty; introduces the
first battery system in South Africa for chickens

1955............... Suffers serious motor vehicle accident but survives
with multiple fractures; visits international health
resorts and clinics; Luigi Cornaro influences change
in lifestyle

1959............... Awarded title of *Cavaliere* (Knight) by Italian
Government

1960............... Lemoenkloof becomes largest poultry farm in
South Africa

1968............... Newcastle Disease hits the Western Cape;
714,000 Lemoenkloof chickens are destroyed
and the farm is quarantined for six months

1968............... Cleto meets Boris Chaitow in the UK

1969............... New beginnings: Lemoenkloof Holding Company
is established.

Saporetti is awarded title of *Commendatore*
(Knight Commander) by Italian Government

1971............... Cleto purchases High Rustenburg Estate in
Stellenbosch; Chaitow arrives from the UK to
establish High Rustenburg Hydro Health Resort

SAPORETTI FAMILY TREE

Carlo Saporetti + Alda Amorati

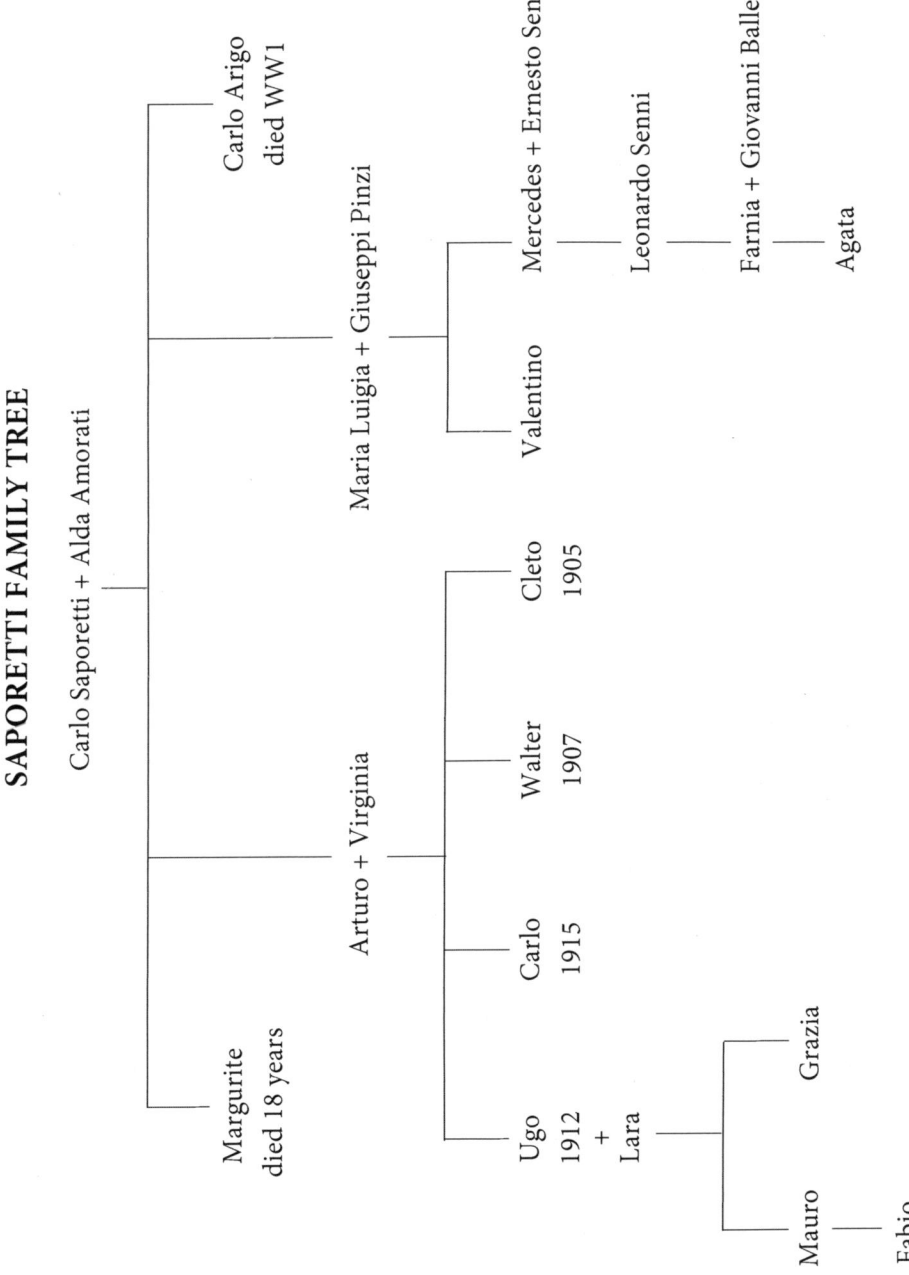

Carlo Arigo died WW1

Maria Luigia + Giuseppi Pinzi

Mercedes + Ernesto Senni

Leonardo Senni

Farnia + Giovanni Ballerini

Agata

Valentino

Margurite died 18 years

Arturo + Virginia

Cleto 1905

Walter 1907

Carlo 1915

Ugo 1912 + Lara

Grazia

Mauro

Fabio

EARLY DAYS
1905–1941

Winter arrived early that year. The wind whistled and howled as the rain lashed against the shutters of the house on 25 Via Baccarini in Ravenna, Italy.

Midwife Filomena Benvenuto tightened the scarf around her neck and hurried past the carriages and late afternoon shoppers on the Piazza Caduti.

Ravenna, with its cobbled streets, brick palaces and spectacular Byzantine mosaics, was home to the Saporetti family. They had established themselves in the historic centre of the town which had once been the capital of the Western Roman Empire. The population in 1900 was about 35,000 mainly middle class citizens. Dante Alighieri, in his *Divine Comedy,* described Ravenna's mosaics as a 'symphony of colour'. Considered the 'Father' of Italian language and known as *Il somma Poeta*, Dante was exiled from his native Florence, and died from malaria in Ravenna, aged 56. His tomb is situated near to the Saporetti residence.

Arturo Saporetti paced back and forth in the salon. From time to time he consulted his pocket watch which had been a gift from his father, Carlo. A handsome and imposing man, Arturo sported lavish sideburns, a well-trimmed moustache and was a serial smoker of evil smelling cheroots. He had managed to capture, with some persuasion, the heart of the beautiful Virginia Zoli. They were both teachers. Married for just over a year, they were nervously expecting the arrival of their first born.

On the 2nd November, 1905, Cleto Saporetti was delivered with minimal fuss and to the considerable delight of his father. Midwife Filomena displayed the lusty infant, while Arturo inspected every nook and cranny of his new son before pronouncing him *perfetto*. In 1905 the Italian economy was booming and Arturo celebrated the birth of his son by treating himself to the new *Fiat Brevetti*, which boasted a top speed of 65 km/hour.

The house on Via Baccarini was spacious and impressive to those viewing it from the street. Arturo and Virginia lived on the upper floor, while Arturo's sister, Maria Luigia, lived on ground level. Her husband Giuseppi Pinzi, originally from nearby San Pietro in Vincoli, was a master coach builder. Also part of the household was Arturo's parents, Carlo and Alda. They too were teachers and had nine children, of whom only four survived. Arturo and Maria Luigia grew to adulthood; Marguerite was one of the 20 million people who died from the Spanish flu, aged 18. Their fourth living child, the dashing young Carlo Arigo, joined the Ravenna regiment in 1916 after Italy declared war on the Austro Hungarian empire. Carlo was much loved and a hero to his family.

At this stage we need to digress from Cleto's story to provide some background to Italy and specifically Ravenna and the Saporetti family during this time.

WWI: La Grande Guerra

Italy wanted to extend her borders to the Dalmatian coastline and acquire Trieste and the Trentino region. War was declared on Austria on 23 May 1915. The frontier was 600 kilometres long, four fifths of it made up of mountains with several mountain peaks being over 3,000 metres high. Italy provided five million soldiers of whom 600,000 perished and another one million wounded. The Austrians fielded an estimated eight million troops. Initial battles were fought at Isonzo and Caporetto, not far from Ravenna. The Italians suffered heavy losses and were severely demoralised. Commander in Chief, General Cadormo, imposed harsh discipline on his troops who he said were "morally unprepared" for war.

He is the only General to have introduced the Roman practice of 'decimation', the killing of every tenth man from units which failed to perform in battle. Many Italians deserted, and in fact the Ravenna brigade mutinied in March 1916. Luckily Cadormo was replaced by the humane General Armando Diaz, who cared for his men and, importantly, increased their food rations. Italian armies could never march on empty stomachs.

The Austrians were confident that they would celebrate Christmas in Venice. Only Monte Grappa remained to be taken. But it was not to be.

Cleto's Uncle Carlo was one of the brave Italian Alpini who shivered in their frozen trenches on the slopes of Monte Grappa, 3,000 metres high. They were outnumbered and outgunned. They faced Austrian flame throwers, trench mortars and gas armed only with their rifles and bayonets. When they ran out of ammunition they hurled grenades and eventually resorted to throwing stones. Many of the Alpini were only 18 years old.

"*Di qui non si passa*" ("From here none shall pass") was the motto of these brave mountain troops. The snow lay up to 12 metres deep in winter. Climbing and skiing were essential skills for troops on both sides. The awful result of explosives was that they set off avalanches. Tens of thousands of soldiers disappeared under the snow. Their bodies were never recovered.

The Italians were ultimately victorious at Vittorio Veneto on 6 November 1918.

Uncle Carlo was one of tens of thousands of young soldiers who perished on the icy slopes of Monte Grappa during World War 1. His name can be seen on the stone memorial erected to commemorate the Ravenna regimental soldiers who lost their lives in *La Grande Guerra*. The memorial is based in the church San Romueldo, which is now The Museo dei Risorgimento Sacrario del Caduti, near to the Saporetti residence in Via Baccarini.

During the war the rest of the Saporetti family moved to Cocciolia, between Forli and Ravenna. Cleto was 10 years old when war was declared. By this stage, he had three younger brothers; Walter, Ugo and Carlo III. A great joy for Arturo to have four sons! Arturo's sister, Maria Luigia, followed suit and added daughter, Mercedes, and a son, Valentino, to the family.

Ravenna 1918, Post War

In 1918, the Saporetti family was able to return to Via Alfredo Baccarini, secure in the knowledge that the mighty Austro-Hungarian empire had crumbled.

However, Italy was now plunged into the misery of post-war years. There was a severe economic crisis. Unemployment, strikes and inflation paved the way for Communist action. Italy was forced to repay four billion gold dollars of wartime loans from America and Britain.

Then in October 1922, Benito Mussolini, known as *Il Duce*, and his followers marched on Rome. The government was powerless. Fascism had arrived and was to dominate Italy for the next two decades. Mussolini's communist party had been formed in 1921 and, by 1925, it had become the sole legal party.

During these hard times many young Italian men made their way overseas, seeking a better life. Amongst these was Vincenzo Ciolli, who arrived in South Africa at the age of 26. Vincenzo and his family were to meet Cleto in 1947, when he started working as a parolee on Dundarach poultry farm near to Klipheuwel in the Western Cape. The Ciollis came from the mountainous Abruzzo region, northeast of Rome. By coincidence, Mussolini was hidden at Gran Sasso in 1943, very close to the Ciolli's family home.

As a young boy, Cleto enjoyed a close friendship with his cousin, Mercedes, and later with her son Leonardo Senni. Mercedes remembers Cleto as being very determined, innovative and an entrepreneur from an early age. He loved being playful and making jokes. At a fancy dress party he arrived dressed as a *Palandrana nera* (undertaker), wearing a long black cloak. This sense of play was to continue throughout his life.

Most Italians were passionate about hunting and Cleto was no exception. He kept his dog Romeo, a handsome, keen-nosed pointer, in the courtyard of his house. Romeo's sworn enemy was Piero, a Macao monkey, who wisely resided out of harm's way on the first floor of the building. On one occasion, Piero escaped and ran away over the roof tops. Hopping through the windows of the Provincial Revenue office, he terrified the astonished ladies whose screams alerted a gallant *Carabaniere* who managed to entice the creature with a slice of fragrant panettone. Sadly, during the brutal winter of 1927, a lonely Piero froze to death when someone left a window open in his room.

While still in his twenties, Cleto formed his own transport company in Ravenna. Confident and enthusiastic, with a warm personality, he was highly intelligent and had received a good education from his parents and grandparents. From 1928 until mid-1930, he worked as a subcontractor for the military division of the Ravenna Garrison, Infantry Division. His supervisor gave a reference which stated: "During this period he followed instructions with diligence and honesty".

From 1931 until December 1934, he subcontracted to road engineer Cesare Bernardi in Ravenna, constructing streets and river embankments. Bernardi reported: "Cleto Saporetti was scrupulously honest, obedient and respectful".

Cleto was later involved in the construction of new main roads in Ravenna. The head of the engineering department in Ravenna,

Il Prefetto, wrote that Cleto had *"Grande competenza ricostruzione delle strade"* (great competence in road reconstruction).

During 1936, he subcontracted to Dr Gaetano Turilli of Trieste to transport motor fuel for the Ravenna military division. During this period, Turilli commented: "Saporetti was an outstanding worker, diligent and honest".

In the meantime, Cleto's younger brothers had also met with some success. Walter, two years younger, joined a bank as a junior staff member. Capable and hardworking, he rose through the ranks to become manager of the *Banca Nazionale del Lavore di Napoli*. He married Iris and went to live in Naples. Walter had no living children.

Carlo Arigo III, the youngest brother, studied dentistry and opened his practice in Forli. Ugo established his own successful business as a dental technician. However, he ran into problems when Italian law ruled that only persons with university qualifications could work in the field of dentistry. Thus Ugo joined brother, Carlo, in his dental practice but there were inevitable disagreements and arguments. Cleto eventually came to the rescue and brought Ugo and his family to Cape Town in 1959.

Hardship hit Cleto's family when it was severely affected by the failure of a grain and cereal factory founded by grandfather, Carlo, and directed by Cleto's father, Arturo. The subsequent bankruptcy was associated with the enormous supplies requisitioned by the army when Italy entered WW2 in 1940. Following the invasion of Ethiopia, state debt had increased dramatically and Italy had extracted forced loans from its citizens. The government was unable to pay for the Saporetti grain.

In those days, the debt was a huge sum. Some of it was honoured by Giuseppi Pinzi, who was married to Cleto's aunt, Maria Luigia. In 1935, Mussolini invaded Ethiopia. He merged Ethiopia with Eritrea and Somalia, declaring that they were part of the Italian Empire. The fact that he used mustard gas on the locals did not endear them to him.

During the thirties, emigration to the colonies was encouraged due to the belief that Italy suffered from 'excess population'. Cleto duly applied to the *Compagnia Italiana per Lavori Nelle Colonie ed all' Estero* which was a society for engineering enterprises overseas. In 1937, he left for Gondar in Ethiopia, former imperial capital, known as the 'Camelot of Africa' due to an abundance of magnificent castles. He was 32 years old and unmarried.

Whilst working as foreman for a construction company, he became ill with malaria. His employer provided a good reference and Cleto moved to Eritrea, attracted by the opportunities offered by this industrial centre and the fact that it was home to many hundreds of companies and other Italians.

WW2 *La seconda Guerra Mondiale*

Meanwhile, Mussolini aimed to expand his Italian Empire by taking land from British and French colonies in North Africa. Italy entered the war in June 1940 and Cleto was conscripted as *Capa Squadra* (sergeant) into the paramilitary 136 Battalion Blackshirts, the *Camicie Nere*.

Italy mobilised the *Cacciatori d'Africa* (Hunters of Africa) and the mobile infantry, or *Bersaglieri*, was joined by the *Pavia* motorised division from Cleto's home town of Ravenna. The Italian Royal Navy, known as the Red Sea Flotilla, had several modern battleships but no aircraft carriers. They occupied the strategic port of Massawa in Eritrea, preventing the allies from using the Suez Canal. The elite mountain troops, the *Alpini*, fought heroic battles on the 2,000 metre high slopes of Amba Alagi. The Italian Royal Air Force had obsolete biplanes compared to the current generation of monoplane fighters of other nations.

During the second battle of *El Alamein* in 1942, the Italians were abandoned by the rest of the Axis forces, and had no option but to surrender. Harry Zinder of *Time* magazine wrote: "The Italians fought well and it was a terrific let down by their German allies". Rommel's Panzer division dissolved, turned tail and left the Italians to fight a rear guard action.

One of the problems encountered by the Italians was the lack of medicines required for endemic diseases. At least a quarter of the troops were suffering from malaria, including the brave and dashing Duc D'Aosta, Governor General of Italian East Africa. He was forced to surrender on the summit of Amba Alagi together with his *Alpini*, outnumbered eight to one by the British forces. Awarded full military honours, he later died from the disease. Revered by his troops, the Duca d'Aosta School was established at Zonderwater POW camp in South Africa some years later.

The port of Massawa was critical to the allies as it allowed them to safely use the Red Sea route to bring supplies to the North African-based medical teams. Rear Admiral Mario Bonetti had been ordered to defend Massawa "to the last man". He was faced with numerically enhanced British forces that were now joined by Indian and South

African troops. The Italians ran out of fuel, ammunition, food and water and were forced to surrender. Before he handed over, Bonetti proceeded to thoroughly wreck the port of Massawa. Access in and out was totally blocked and the harbour was rendered useless for more than a year. At least 24 ships were scuttled, blocking the entrance. Four Italian submarines managed to sneak out. Making their way down the coast of East Africa, they rounded the Cape of South Africa, eventually arriving in the safe haven of France. As a parting shot, they torpedoed the British cruiser, HMS Cape Town. Badly damaged, she had to be towed to Bombay for repairs.

Cleto joined almost 100,000 Italian POWs at Massawa. The British had no means of feeding them and decided to send them to South Africa. They were transported by ship to Durban, then by train to Pretoria and Zonderwater prison. Cleto became POW 258419 and was to stay at Zonderwater until he was released on parole 5 years later, in 1947.

Fortunately Cleto had not been allocated to the Nova Scotia carrying 780 POWs to South Africa, as it was torpedoed off the coast of Durban by Kapitan Lieutenant Robert Gysae, commander of the German submarine U-177. Gysae had mistakenly identified the ship as an enemy cruiser under camouflage and heavily armed. The Nova Scotia was nothing of the sort. She sank within eight minutes with the loss of almost 700 Italians who drowned or were taken by sharks. Commander Gysae had made a horrendous error of judgement.

POW Giuseppi Chisin also missed being transported on the Nova Scotia, because it was fully loaded. He arrived at Zonderwater, where he met Cleto, and later worked with him at Lemoenkloof, remaining there for almost 30 years.

Orlando Valacchi, who was captured at Tobruk, was sent first to India as a POW, then on to Durban and Zonderwater where he met Cleto and later became part of the Italian team who worked with Cleto at Lemoenkloof.

Meanwhile, all support for Mussolini in Italy evaporated when Sicily was invaded by the Allies. He was deposed, arrested, and then dramatically rescued by German paratroopers from Gran Sasso in the Abruzzi mountains where he had been hidden by the Allies. The Italian government secretly signed an armistice with the Allies on September 8th, 1943.

The contribution of Italian anti-fascists in the campaign has largely been forgotten over the years. Partisans depended on arms and supplies parachuted to them by the British SOE (Special Operations Executive) and the American OSS (Office of Strategic Services, which later became the CIA). 20-year-old Mino Farneti, from Cleto's home town of Ravenna, set up a secret radio hidden in a beehive, south of the city, aiding the Allies with their tactics against the Germans. Another young man from Ravenna, code-named "Bulow", came up with an audacious plan. Together with the 28th Garabaldi Brigade of partisans, the Allied troops, and Popsky's private army of elite commandoes, they convinced the Germans to retreat, leaving Ravenna intact.

PRISONERS OF WAR, ZONDERWATER 1941–1947

There never was a good war or a bad peace.

(Benjamin Franklin)

Vast numbers of Italians were taken *Prigionieri di Guerra,* Prisoners of War, in North and East Africa during the period 1941–1943. There were almost 100,000 of them, many still teenagers. The British were faced with the problem of how to feed and accommodate them. War-ravaged Europe and the UK were not an option, as it was too dangerous to sail in the Mediterranean. Because of the menace of submarine activity, it was decided to send the officers to India, and the rest of the men down the east coast to South Africa.

Travelling by ship they made their way over rough seas, huddled in the hold, many becoming violently seasick, until they reached Durban which was the main port of Natal. From there they were transferred onto trains and guarded by ferocious-looking Zulus armed with *assegais* (spears). South Africa was an unknown country to most of the prisoners who were young *contadini,* or farm workers, most of whom could not speak English and many of whom were illiterate. Prowling along the coast of southern Africa were the

German U-boats, undersea predators who had sunk an estimated 49 Allied ships within a thousand miles of the coast, including the Nova Scotia in 1942.

To say that the South Africans were unprepared for this avalanche of prisoners is an understatement. Confusion reigned. Zonderwater, near to Cullinan and just outside Pretoria, was the designated destination. It was to become the largest Allied prisoner of war camp of WW2. In 1941, 10,000 prisoners arrived, followed by 54,000 in 1942, and another 63,000 in 1943. They were mainly privates and non-commissioned officers. At a later stage, external camps were established where prisoners could work on farms and construction sites. This took care of about 20,000 prisoners, with camps at Du Toit's Kloof, Paarl, Worcester, and Wellington in the Western Cape, with some additional camps in Natal.

On arrival, Italians and South African staff faced each other with some degree of trepidation. Most of the Italians did not speak English, or Afrikaans, for that matter. It was a challenge to communicate. Almost 9,000 Italians were illiterate. However, out of chaos eventually came order.

The camp began as a massive tent town which evolved into solid huts constructed from bricks, concrete and corrugated iron. Making the best use of their skills, the Italians provided most of the labour. The Geneva Convention of 1929 had laid down minimal conditions of detention by the detaining power. With Switzerland as the protecting power and also the International Red Cross, a watching brief was maintained at all times to see that the minimum standards were observed. Zonderwater became the best POW facility in the world at that time, and even today is recognised as a remarkable achievement.

Much of the success was due to the administration of the camp commander, Colonel Hendrik Frederick Prinsloo, eldest son of Spioenkop and Boer war hero, Commandant H.F. Prinsloo. He treated the prisoners with respect and understood their feelings of abandonment and isolation. Recognising their talents and skills, he nurtured and utilised these strengths to create an establishment that the Italians were proud of. Initially the prisoners, who were generally feeling negative, spent their days planning their escape. But with Prinsloo's initiative, Zonderwater was transformed into a vibrant and viable establishment.

There were 14 blocks in total, each comprising four camps. In addition, there was a transit camp, two disinfestation camps and a hospital which had some 1,600 beds, making it the largest bedded hospital in South Africa. The hospital was staffed by Union Defence Force members and Italian POW medical officers. It was a model for POW camps everywhere. With the best equipment and operating theatres, the medical staff were able to tackle most surgical and medical problems. Each block had its own clinic where day-to-day ailments were handled by an Italian POW medical doctor, and more serious cases were referred to the main hospital. Without doubt, the majority of Italians did not have this degree of care and expertise in their home country at that time.

Hygiene challenges were successfully overcome by means of an efficient sewerage system. Cariflocculators were built for waste water treatment.

An area of about 35 hectares of irrigated land and 250 hectares of unirrigated land, which had previously been regarded as unproductive, was put under the expert supervision of a UDF officer with agricultural experience. The Italians set to with gusto, looking forward to harvesting bumper crops of delicious vegetables. Culinary skills were promoted and meal times, which were always enjoyed, formed a basis of camaraderie which was lacking, and possibly unheard of, in other POW camps. With statues and fountains constructed in the grounds, this section of South Africa began to look like an Italian village.

The Italians were mostly Roman Catholic and their needs were administered by 23 POW priests. Several chapels were built and beautifully decorated with murals.

A major achievement was the implementation of education and literacy programmes. At least 9,000 illiterate POWs were taught to read and write in their mother tongue. The main school was named after their hero, Amedeo Duca d'Aosta, Governor General of Italian East Africa. It is claimed that Saporetti wrote a book while in Zonderwater but, if he did, it has never been found.

Having been farm workers when taken prisoner, some 5,000 POWs learned new trades. Instruction in carpentry was held at the H.F. Prinsloo vocational centre, and classes in technical drawing included the manufacture of class aids and tools, by the students themselves, as part of their training. At least 15 schools were established and maintained in the blocks. A central library was built and stocked, while each block had its own branch library.

One of the POWs, Orlando Valacchi, born in Milan in 1920, is of interest. After meeting Saporetti in the camp, he spent some time as a parolee, then later joined Lemoenkloof Enterprises, meeting and socialising with Cleto's friends and clients. Valacchi, a former professional cyclist, was captured at El Alamein in 1943. Sent to Zonderwater via India, he became a good friend of Cleto's. Released on parole in 1947, he was sent to Wellington to join eight other POWs. Orlando recalls that they were "very rough Southerners". He was designated cook for this group, but pursued his loved for cycling by exploring the beautiful countryside. Meeting up with some fellow Italians who worked on a nearby poultry farm, he was instructed in a method of appropriating chickens by climbing through a vulnerable area in the perimeter of the farm. Orlando's group henceforth enjoyed many chicken dinners. *Pollo alla cacciatore* was a favourite, as well as *pollo al forno*, and occasionally *petti di pollo alla Milanese.*

On one occasion he visited a group of POWs working at Bainskloof; they were constructing the road over this magnificent mountain pass. The men had been given large amounts of tea by the International Red Cross. However, Italians do not drink tea. "No problem," grinned Orlando, displaying some impressive steel teeth. "I will help you!" Back in Wellington he presented the grateful and unsuspecting poultry farmer with a gift of tea. He presented the Bainskloof Italians with a basket of chickens. Everyone was happy.

Some years later, Orlando met up with Cleto, in Cape Town. By this time, Saporetti owned the restaurants *El Pescatore* in Mouille Point, *Coq d'Or* in Long Street, and *La Perla* in Waterkant Street. The original *La Perla* was purchased by young Emiliano Sandri, who went on to open the highly successful and popular *La Perla* in Sea Point, together with two more restaurants in the southern suburbs, and Stellenbosch. Many politicians and celebrities ate at *El Pescatore,* where Orlando first met Professor Chris Barnard of heart-transplant fame. Emiliano Sandri introduced Barnard to Rome's leading tailor, Angelo Litrico. Litrico counted the Pope, Kruschev, the Kennedy's Juan Peron, King Hussein, and various movie stars amongst his customers. Sandri recalls: "Barnard was like a god in Italy". Litrico had a close friendship with Barnard and later sponsored dozens of children to be treated by Barnard in Cape Town. The Italian patients and their families stayed with Orlando in his Woodstock home where he kept them happy with gnocchi, homemade tagliatelli, and proper espresso.

Sport at the camp was of major importance. Football, tennis, *bocce* (bowls) and *pallavolo* (basketball) grounds were built for each block. Athletic competitions were held. Football league and boxing tournaments were organised regularly, controlled by a UDF sports officer together with his Italian POW counterpart. Boxers, Fortunato Manca and Gino Verdinelli, drew large crowds when they contested the official Italian Middleweight title at Zonderwater.

Music and theatre were an important cultural part of camp life. Each block had its own theatre company. All scenario costumes and lighting were improvised by the POWs. Costumes were created from sacking, and even cotton wool was used to simulate fur, with a resultant decline in the medical stores. Operettas such as *La Principessa degli Zingari* (The Merry Widow) and *Il paese dei Campanelli* (Maid of the Mountains) were performed with great enthusiasm. Musical shows were keenly attended and make-up artists transformed performers to be included in the 'female' chorus. *O sole Mio* and *Volare* reverberated in the showers. Numerous small orchestras performed classical and popular music of a high standard, and a symphony orchestra of about 90 musicians was created in addition to a brass and woodwind band.

Medical care in the camp was of the highest possible standards. There was scrupulous cleanliness in the kitchens and ablution blocks. All new arrivals were de-loused, all men were vaccinated and re-vaccinated against smallpox and inoculated against typhoid. Food was inspected daily by food inspectors. All drinking water was purified. Modern sewerage disposal was established.

Between 1942 and 1943, there were almost 500,000 visits to clinics. Of these, 11,000 cases were admitted to hospital. There were 56 deaths, which amounted to 0.005 per cent mortality, despite the influx of diseases such as amoebic dysentery, tuberculosis, and malaria.

The resistance to illness and enhancement of the immune system was greatly strengthened by a generous balanced diet of 3,000 calories per day. According to the Red Cross statistics, South African POWs in Germany received 2,000 calories per day, while in Italy they were given about 1,000 calories daily. At Zonderwater, the men were able to supplement their diet by using their monthly pay to purchase additional foods available at canteens in all the blocks.

Colonel Blumberg listed a number of beneficial facts which contributed to the wellbeing of the prisoners. Most of them were from sturdy stock with an average age of 25. Cleto was a mature 37. They had limited amounts of alcohol and tobacco. They had an excellent diet and plenty of time for sport and recreation, including creative activities. Their self-esteem and self-worth increased when they received education and training at the camp schools.

It is a tribute to Colonel Prinsloo, Camp Commandant, and his team of UDF personnel, that after six years of captivity, the POWs returned to their native land in no way traumatised by their experience. On the contrary, for many these had been useful and educational years. They returned as healthy individuals, both physically and emotionally. Many POWs requested permanent residence in South Africa and 850 permits were granted. Saporetti was one of those allowed to remain. Later, another 20,000 Italians were allowed to return to South Africa.

Saporetti was released to Captain J.A. Ball and granted South African residence in January 1947. The camp was closed in February 1947.

Colonel Prinsloo and Captain Ball were invested with the Order of the Star of Italy by the post-war Italian government. Further recognition came when His Holiness the Pope conferred upon Colonel Prinsloo the *Ordine di Bene Merente,* which is the Papal decoration, the Order of Good Merit.

LEMOENKLOOF
1950–1980

From small beginnings come great things.
(Proverb)

The next phase of Cleto's life was about to begin. And also his destiny.

Many of the POWs released from Zonderwater in 1947 returned to Italy. Cleto chose to stay and relocated to Dundarach poultry farm in Klipheuwel. This was, and still is, a farming area in the Western Cape between Paarl and Malmesbury, about 50 kms from Cape Town. The agreement signed with owner Alistair Stuart provided Cleto with "Free board and lodging, a monthly wage of 20 pounds, and a bonus of four pounds per 1,000 chicks reared by him to the age of one month with a mortality rate not exceeding five per cent".

Living not far from Dundarach farm was the Ciolli family. The Ciollis had moved to the Cape from Natal, and now had a major contract supplying crushed stone to fill in the Cape Town foreshore and dock area. Every Sunday Cleto visited the Ciollis. Arriving on his motorbike, he joined the family in a typical Italian feast. Remarked Vicenzo Ciolli: "Cleto was no rough diamond. He was a real gentleman".

Close to Dundarach was another poultry farm, the 200-hectare Lemoenkloof owned by Ben Godfrey. Ben asked Alistair Stuart if he could recommend a good manager for his farm, which was not in good shape. "I've got just the person for you," replied Stuart. "Saporetti is hardworking, intelligent and eager to learn".

Thus Cleto arrived at Lemoenkloof, rolled up his sleeves and set to work. He was 45-years-old. Within a short time he was confident that poultry farming could be highly profitable. Cleto received no pay for some time and eventually Ben Godfrey announced: "I must owe you almost 1,000 pounds in salary. I am afraid that I cannot pay you, but if you take over the bond on the farm, it is yours."

This was a challenge for Cleto who had just 50 pounds in his pocket. He offered Godfrey nine post-dated cheques to pay for Lemoenkloof over a period of years. One can still see those cheques today, framed and on display inside the Lemoenkloof offices. It is a compliment to the integrity of Saporetti that Ben Godfrey accepted these conditions.

In the early days, chickens were kept in runs. Cleto decided to install a battery system for his poultry, finding this to be a far more efficient way of monitoring and controlling them. He was the first to do so in South Africa, although the practice was soon adopted by other poultry farmers.

One of Cleto's dictums was "to cut out the middle man" and so he set up his own distribution centre in Maitland. All eggs were sent there, with the surplus going to wholesalers. Another of his dictums was "do not waste anything". Feathers from slaughtered birds were dried and sold. Droppings from every battery were collected, dried and sold as garden manure. They were also used to fertilise a nursery where he grew vegetables, carnations and cyclamens.

He employed 14 European families, each provided with a house and a subsidised car. All single men ate their midday meal at Cleto's rambling, Cape Dutch-styled house which was built in 1863. The long dining table was laden with steaming bowls of pasta, spaghetti or tagliatelli with *ragu* or *polpette*, occasional polenta, minestrone in winter, fresh vegetables and fruit from the garden, homemade bread, local cheeses, a glass of *Vino Rosso* and some strong espresso to end the meal. On weekends there would be *stufato di Manzo* (beef casserole) or perhaps *costolette di maiale* (pork chops). Every Sunday evening was 'movie night'. Cleto's nephew, Mauro, operated the projector and the nostalgic Italians enjoyed watching Rossano Brazzi and other Italian movie stars. Torro, the parrot, was Cleto's pet. He hated everyone apart from his master. When Cleto took Torro to the farm offices, the staff kept well away.

In addition, there were approximately 180 farm contract workers. Cleto ensured that "No man is ever given too much work to do. Each person has his fair share and no more". It is no wonder that Lemoenkloof employees were loyal and happy. Those that remain today, specifically the children of fathers who worked on the farm, recall an idyllic lifestyle and likened it to an Italian village.

Each month a braai (barbeque) was held for the entire staff. Boerewors (sausage) was always popular, while wives supplied the salads. A crèche was established and a hall made available for church services. Friday was shopping day, when the farm minibus took staff members to nearby Paarl.

In 1950, when Cleto arrived at Lemoenkloof, there were 6,000 chickens. By 1958, numbers had increased to 60,000.

Ben Godfrey had a sister, Letty, who left her parents in Piketberg to assist Ben with bookkeeping at Lemoenkloof. She was tiny, energetic and bubbly, and well-liked by all who met her. It was not long before Cleto asked her to be his wife. He had never been married before. They were both 49 years old and enjoyed a very happy marriage which lasted for 20 years until Letty's death from cancer in 1974.

Brian Wilson, Boris Chaitow's stepson, met Letty in 1972. He had this to say about her: "Cleto and Letty were fun to be around. People acknowledged Cleto on every street corner. Letty was amazingly kind and involved me in her life going swimming and surfing, even baking bread. Her staff all loved her. When we visited Cape Town, she would fill up her old Mercedes with flowers from their garden, and drop them off to various flower sellers by the roadside. My final memory of Cleto at High Rustenburg Hydro was when he presided at a function flamboyantly dressed with a frilly lampshade on his head".

Emiliano Sandri recalls an occasion when Cleto and Letty were visiting his home in Cape Town. The beautiful strains of Bellini's opera *La Straniera* prompted Cleto to get down on one knee before his wife while he proceeded to sing the words to her. It was a special, moving moment and one that Sandri never forgot.

When Letty died, she left funds in her estate to be utilised to assist the elderly. She also made bequests to her nieces and nephews on the condition that they "changed their habits". Willy de Villiers, as executor, wondered how he could monitor this!

Michelina Pacifica Ciman spent many happy days on Lemoenkloof as a child. Her father, Liberio, was in charge of the small chicks. Her mother, Filomena, was an excellent cook and Cleto often dropped by to enjoy her *Risotto Milanese* and *Pannacotta*. Michelina is now married to the owner of the popular *La Masseria* restaurant in Stellenbosch.

Cleto employed many former POWs on the farm. Giuseppi Chisin and Antonio Caputo were captured at Tobruk and sent as POWs to Zonderwater, then subsequently sent to work on farms in the Western Cape. In 1950 they joined Cleto at Lemoenkloof, where they remained for many years.

Another former POW captured at El Alamein was Orlando Valacchi who went on to construct refrigerated facilities in Maitland which were used as a depot for the distribution of Lemoenkloof produce. Orlando came to Lemoenkloof after working as a parolee in Wellington on the farm "Welbedacht", now owned by Emiliano Sandri.

He recalls: "Cleto was a gentleman and helped a lot of people". Orlando married Edna Viola from Veldrif in the North Western Cape. His brother, Romano Valacchi, also worked for Cleto, transporting chickens to the Maitland depot.

The chickens at Lemoenkloof were 'first cross' Black Australorp hens crossed with white Leghorn cockerels. In Cleto's home town, the dual-purpose breed of chicken, known as Romagnola, has become almost extinct in recent years, but is now recovering, although the Romagnola have not been introduced into South Africa. Cleto experimented with his chicken's feed in the hope of improving the quality and quantity of their eggs. He found that only a certain amount of protein was acceptable, as increased protein content did not increase the number of eggs. He then introduced highly nutritious lucerne into their feed, but when their feathers turned pink, he was obliged to stop. In order to study his poultry, people say that in the early days he actually slept with the baby chicks.

Soon after Saporetti introduced his battery system, it was noticed that a number of eggs were produced with poor quality shells. Several of the cockerels had crooked breast bones. It was found that about 6,000 chickens varying in ages from four to eight weeks were suffering from Vitamin D deficiency. This was a result of the chickens being accommodated in batteries, under corrugated sheet covering, deprived of direct sunshine. The Vitamin D deficiency occurred even though the chickens were being fed with cod liver oil in recommended amounts.

It is a credit to Saporetti that he called in a scientist to investigate the problem. Dr A.C. Roux found that even chickens that had been exposed to sunlight experienced only a small increase in Vitamin D, whereas the addition of synthetic Vitamin D to the feed increased the Vitamin D content of the eggs threefold.

The next step was to test the cod liver oil which Cleto was feeding his chickens. It was concluded that the destruction of Vitamin D was caused by prolonged storage of the oil in 45 gallon drums in direct sunlight. Cleto added synthetic Vitamin D3 in powder form to his mash. Within a few days the lethargic chicks became more energetic and within two weeks, the battery was too confined for their vigorous romping.

Research into the matter, conducted by Dr Roux, was subsequently published in the *World's Poultry Science Journal*, 1957.

Through conducting the experiments with feeding his chickens, Cleto became interested in nutrition.

Earlier, in 1955, Cleto had almost lost his life. While driving his Oldsmobile over dirt roads he was forced to swerve to avoid a stray dog. The car skidded and rolled. Taken to Paarl hospital with multiple fractures and severe concussion, it was feared that Cleto would never walk again. In fact, 27 bones had sustained fractures. With Letty's help he eventually limped back to Lemoenkloof, and slowly repaired his broken body. It was at this stage that he was introduced to the philosophy of 'Nature Cure' and was particularly influenced by the findings of Luigi Cornaro.

Luigi Cornaro (1467–1565) was a Venetian nobleman. He wrote his book *How to Live One Hundred Years* when he was 85 years old. Luigi had been eating and drinking in excess, with the resulting deranged digestive system and serious ill health by the age of 35. Feasting and gluttony were the order of the day in the 15th century and overeating was considered a social privilege. In those days, doctors believed in bloodletting and purging, and also consulted the stars for guidance.

Cornaro's conversion to a simple diet and exercise was a last resort. Within a year he had regained his health. He wrote that "eating little makes a man live very long". Today, many centuries later, modern science has come to the same conclusion as it has been shown that calorie restriction increases longevity. Cornaro ate only 400 grams of food daily. This included bread, fish, meat, eggs and soup. He did not, however, eliminate wine and allowed himself a generous 450 ml or three wine glasses of red wine daily.

After Cleto's conversion to Cornaro's philosophy, he always carried a bottle of carrot and beetroot juice in his car. However, Cleto was not a total convert! At Lemoenkloof he visited the Caputo and Pacifico homes to enjoy the excellent cuisine. Rosa Caputo was famous for her lasagne. "Don't tell anyone," whispered Cleto when he departed after each visit. On his many trips to Italy he enjoyed, in full, the cooking of his family; there were many happy occasions filled with fun and laughter while in Ravenna, Riccione, Naples, Monteverde and Monte Fiori.

After his accident, Cleto visited a number of international health centres and clinics, but it was his meeting with naturopath Boris Chaitow, in the UK, that clarified and motivated his desire to establish a health centre in South Africa.

In 1959, the Italian government awarded Saporetti the title of *Cavaliere* (Knight). Looking back to his arrival at Lemoenkloof nine years earlier with no capital and only 50 pounds in his pocket, it is remarkable that he achieved great success in such a short period. Not only was he sole owner of Lemoenkloof, he also owned three restaurants, a pet shop, a garden shop and a health shop under the Parkade in Cape Town.

When interviewed by a journalist, seven years after he had purchased Lemoenkloof, he was asked how it was possible to achieve such success in so short a time. "Just by making up your mind what you want to do and doing it," stated Cleto, slapping his trouser pockets. "I have nothing in my pockets but my credit is good".

Ten years later, Cleto received the additional title of *Commendatore* (Knight Commander) which was an extraordinary honour. In full, this was *Commendatore dell'ordine al merito della Republica Italiana* (Commander of the Order of Merit of the Italian Republic).

1959 was a busy year. Cleto brought his brother Ugo, wife Lara, and children Mauro and Grazia, to live at Lemoenkloof. Ugo ran the farm shop for some time, and then moved with his family to Sea Point, in Cape Town.

Willy de Villiers joined Lemoenkloof in 1960 and was a major part of its future success. As a young man during WW2, Willy had been given the extremely dangerous task of manufacturing mustard gas in a factory near to Firgrove, about 50 kms outside of Cape Town. Thousands of tons of gas were stored in steel drums. With Willy standing guard, they were transported by train to Port Elizabeth, via Noupoort, a long inland route so as to avoid the German submarines prowling along the coast. It was deemed too dangerous to produce mustard gas in the UK because of the danger of bombing. Willy recalls eating bully beef and biscuits in a first class carriage, accompanied by several soldiers for protection. Sandbags were packed between the drums. While Willy was busy producing mustard gas, Cleto was part of the *Camicie Nere* in Eritrea facing the combined forces of British, South African and Indian army troops.

After the war Willy joined a modest poultry farm owned by Dr Finlayson. Called "Kelvin Grove", it was situated in Constantia. Dr Finlayson's sons later established the enormously successful Glen Carlou Wine estate in the Cape winelands.

Willy came to Lemoenkloof with its 60,000 chickens and described their operation as 'vertically integrated'. Chicken feed mixed with vitamins was created on the farm. A distribution depot for eggs and chickens was established in Maitland. Willy describes Cleto as "a wonderful gentleman and an entrepreneur – I learned a great deal about business from him".

It was during these years that Cleto met young Emiliano Sandri and they became good friends. Sandri purchased the *La Perla* restaurant in Waterkant Street, Cape Town, and then opened the glamorous new version in Sea Point. Cleto was a frequent guest and was proud of Emiliano's achievements. On a recent visit to Cape Town, Orlando Valacchi, now in his nineties and still vigorous and sprightly, visited Cleto's restaurant *El Pescatore* in Mouille Point where, in the past, politicians and well-known businessmen met. At the time of writing, it still exists and is now called *Theo's*.

Disaster: Newcastle Disease hits the Western Cape

The year was 1968. Cleto, with the help of Willy de Villiers, had increased the chicken population at Lemoenkloof to over 700,000. Saporetti was possibly the largest poultry farmer in South Africa. The farm was running smoothly. The staff was happy and contented. The chickens were well fed and well cared for. Scrupulous hygiene was adhered to. All birds were vaccinated, then injected, and subsequently every four-week-old chick was also injected. He had worked hard for 17 years at Lemoenkloof. Cleto was starting to think about his vision of creating a health centre and promoting health to the people of South Africa.

But then disaster struck. No-one was able to identify the origin, but suddenly chickens on the farm started coughing. Strange head twisting (known as torticollis), paralysis and sudden death occurred. Misshapen eggs were laid. To Cleto's and Willy's horror, Newcastle Disease was diagnosed.

Newcastle Disease, a highly contagious viral disease affecting birds – specifically poultry – was first recognised in the UK in 1926. Spread by direct contact between birds, and transmitted by bird droppings, it spreads rapidly in confined areas such as batteries, and is invariably fatal. There is no cure, but prophylactic vaccines may be given. Poultry must be quarantined. Even though birds are inoculated it is still possible to contract the infection. The disease is not hazardous to humans, but creates mild flu-like symptoms, or mild conjunctivitis.

The entire farm was placed under quarantine. A letter from Cleto to his customers was sent as follows:

> *"It is with regret that we have to advise you that as from Monday 8th April, 1968, we shall not be able to supply you for an indefinite period with our quality eggs and poultry. This sad state of affairs has come to being through us being put under strict quarantine measures by the State Department of Veterinary Services because of a suspected outbreak of Newcastle Disease on our farm, notwithstanding all precautions taken by ourselves and the department. However it is our firm intention to overcome this temporary setback and to continue to be of service to you in the very near future with, if possible, poultry and eggs of an even higher standard than in the past".*

However, all efforts were in vain, and the decision was taken to exterminate all 714,000 chickens. One by one, all his carefully nurtured chickens were thrown into trenches, covered with diesel and set alight. Cleto could not bear to watch the proceedings or to hear the squawking and screaming of these doomed birds as they were flung into a fiery and evil-smelling grave. He took his car and drove off to some unknown place and did not return for some time.

Although the authorities were not sure, the 'Cape Doctor' – the famous South Easterly wind – was blamed for the spread of the disease which had originated in and spread from Kuilsriver.

During the subsequent six-month quarantine period, two inspectors lived on the farm to monitor the comprehensive cleaning process. All the buildings were washed down with caustic soda. A short while later, when Cleto had overcome his grief and had recovered his incredible optimism, he told a despondent Willy de Villiers: "I came into this country with nothing. If I leave with nothing, I have lost nothing".

In a remarkable letter to his 400 staff and their families, dated 11th April, he wrote, and also read out to the sombre and apprehensive gathering:

> *"Dear Friends,*
>
> *I called all of you here today because I felt it was time to tell you my feelings after the fate which struck Lemoenkloof this month.*
>
> *First of all I must thank you very much for your support in this difficult moment, and your sympathy towards my wife and myself.*
>
> *I must confess that for the first few days I was overwhelmed by this sad event, so probably I was hurt morally, physically and, not the least, financially. But suddenly I recovered and for the last few days I have become normal.*
>
> *Always I said and reckoned that a business man, small or big, to be able to be called so, must be able to overcome any difficulty in business, and not only to smile when he puts into*

his pocket a few thousand rands, but also when he loses a few hundred thousand of them.

Unfortunately at this very stage it is difficult for me to see clearly when and how we are going to start again, as too much work still lies ahead of us, and to be done.

For the present I wish to thank you all very much for your faithful service in the past, and co-operation and understanding in the present circumstances. I feel also to say it, and openly that all of us owe to our general manager Mr Willy de Villiers, our gratitude and respect for the magnificent job he has done, to see that the badly damaged ship could reach the dockyard safely so as to enable us to assess the damage and, if and how, eventually to be repaired.

On this sad occasion and nevertheless, I propose to toast to the health of ourselves, our families and friends, and not the least, for the future of Lemoenkloof.

Thank you again and deep regards to you all. Good luck!

Cleto Saporetti".

Many letters of sympathy were sent by customers, suppliers, and other poultry organisations. Raymond Ackerman, who had recently established the Pick 'n Pay supermarket chain, wrote this letter to Cleto:

"I heard last week of the disaster which had struck your chicken farm and I cannot tell you how sorry I was to hear of what has happened. I hope that the restriction on your farm is only temporary and that you will soon be on your feet again".

Another letter from Noddy Grinstead from Du Toit's Kloof poultry farm in Paarl, read:

"Knowing you as an exceptional man of great courage and fortitude we know that you will rescue the position and solve your immense difficulties in the spirit that only Cleto Saporetti can display".

A letter from the SA Poultry Association was received in June:

"We of the SA Poultry Association would like to express our sympathy, but words are inadequate in a situation such as this. What struck us most is the fact that you are without rancour and recrimination and, if we may be permitted to say so, this is to us who have the privilege of knowing you, so typical of your character, Thank you for giving us the opportunity of learning from you how one should react to such extremely devastating circumstances".

Cleto also wrote to his former employers at Dundarach poultry farm.

"Dear Mr and Mrs Alistair Stuart,

Today I am another man as at least and at last the mass slaughtering has terminated, as well as the roaring of the bulldozer engaged to dig deep trenches everywhere.

What a peace!

Tomorrow we are sending away the first batch of 90 Bantu, tickets paid, and pocket money.

It was really consoling and nice of you to remember me and my wife on this sad occasion and we thank you for your kind words.

I can assure you that except for a couple of days in which I was probably caught emotionally and consequently also a little physically, very quickly I gain control of myself and now everything is a memory of the past, and I am looking forward to seeing what is more convenient for me to do.

Fortunately I have no debts, am in good health, and good loser, as it is the third time I have lost money. I am an expert.

I sincerely hope that Newcastle disease will spare you.

From my wife, self, good luck and health

Sappo".

During the six-month quarantine period, Willy de Villiers was delegated to sell Lemoenkloof. He travelled around South Africa but nobody was interested; the asking price was R600,000 including all equipment and machinery. Cleto told Willy: "Willy don't worry, you stay with me even if we have to sell". On 1st August, 1968, Lemoenkloof was declared clean. However, starting from scratch was not easy. Eventually a solution was found and The Lemoenkloof Holding Company was formed. Cleto held 50 per cent of the company and the remaining 50 per cent was taken up by Willy, Letty, Antonio Caputo, Giuseppi Chisin, Cleto's brother Ugo, and others.

Starting from ground zero, Willy and Cleto bought day-old chicks and some pullets three to four months old, and just starting to lay. They were also cross Australorp/Leghorn. Julian Mirvish of Tokai Poultry had taken over Dr Finlayson's poultry farm some time previously. Mirvish had a talent for marketing. His motto was "Tokai CHIX lay the best eggs". Mirvish supplied Cleto with Tokai chix and very soon Lemoenkloof was back in business.

Adjacent to Lemoenkloof was Blydskap, a 1,200 hectare, neglected and poorly-developed farm. It had vines, but the soil was poor. But Blydskap had something which Cleto needed. Water!! During the summer months, fierce sun beat down on the roofs of the battery chickens. Cleto aimed to cool them down by spraying water overhead. Blydskap was purchased for R200,000 in 1973.

Cleto owned another farm, Vrederust, in Paarl. Formerly Du Toit's Kloof poultry, its previous owner was Signor Farinella. Vrederust was incorporated into Lemoenkloof Holdings. Lemoenkloof continued to thrive and flourish and was sold, along with Vrederust, to Bokomo in 1980 for R2,5 million.

Within a year of the Lemoenkloof Holding Company's formation, the company showed a profit of R100,000, and after two years, another R100,000. They now had 300,000 chickens. After four years, a total of R600,000 profit was shown, equal to the purchase price of the farm. Cleto still retained 50 per cent of the holding company, but Lemoenkloof itself was no longer his and he was heartsore at losing his farm. Willy hosted a party for 300 people at the fancy Van Donk Club on top of the Trust Bank building in Cape Town. Everyone in the poultry industry attended, but Cleto stayed away.

At the time of writing this book, the CEO and sole owner of Lemoenkloof is Dirk Serdyn. The farm of 220 hectares has many new buildings, and houses 600,000 chickens. Serdyn markets only eggs from this farm. The original name of Lemoenkloof has, for certain legal requirements, been changed to *Amaganda*, which is Xhosa for Egg.

With the successful renaissance and subsequent sale of Lemoen-kloof to his partners, Cleto started looking for a suitable estate where he could fulfil his dream of establishing a health farm. He acquired High Rustenburg Estate in 1971 and invested so much of his capital into this venture that Willy de Villiers called it "The Golden Hill". Cleto now divided his time between his flat in Sea Point, and a house in Stellenbosch. However, once the Hydro was established, Cleto enjoyed staying in a caravan on the property.

Cleto Saporetti

Cleto and younger
brother Walter,
Ravenna, 1910.

Arturo Saporetti,
Cleto's father.

SANSONI GIULIO
SANSONI GIULIO DI GIUSEPPE
SANSONI MATTEO
SANTANDREA GIOVANNI
SAPORETTI ARRIGO
SAPORETTI NATALE
SAPORETTI EMILIO TERZO

Cleto's uncle Carlo Arrigo perished on Monte Grappa WW1, 1916.

Museo dei Risorgimento Sacrario dei Caduti (museum dedicated to the fallen soldiers), Ravenna.

Ravenna Regiment WW1 – "Italia libero dio lo vuole" (free Italy with God's help).

Funeral procession in Ravenna for Carlo Arrigo and other brave WW1 soldiers.

Cleto aged 20 years joins the military.

Above and top right: Cleto and fellow members of the 2nd Alpine regiment at the Vittorio Emanuele barracks in Florence.

Leonardo Senni, Cleto's nephew, present owner of Saporetti's home.

7th Generation of Saporetti family live at 25 Via Baccarini, Ravenna.

Cleto joins the Camicie Nere (Black Shirts), Eritrea, 1940.

Arrival of 100,000 Italian prisoners of war at Zonderwater POW Camp, Cullinan, South Africa.

Boxing matches at Zonderwater were popular.

POWs enjoyed musicals, theatre, and opera in the camp.

Repatriation of Italian POWs from Zonderwater, 1947.

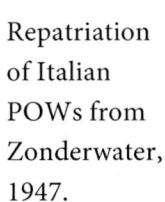

Memorial service at Zonderwater, 2012, for Italian POWs.

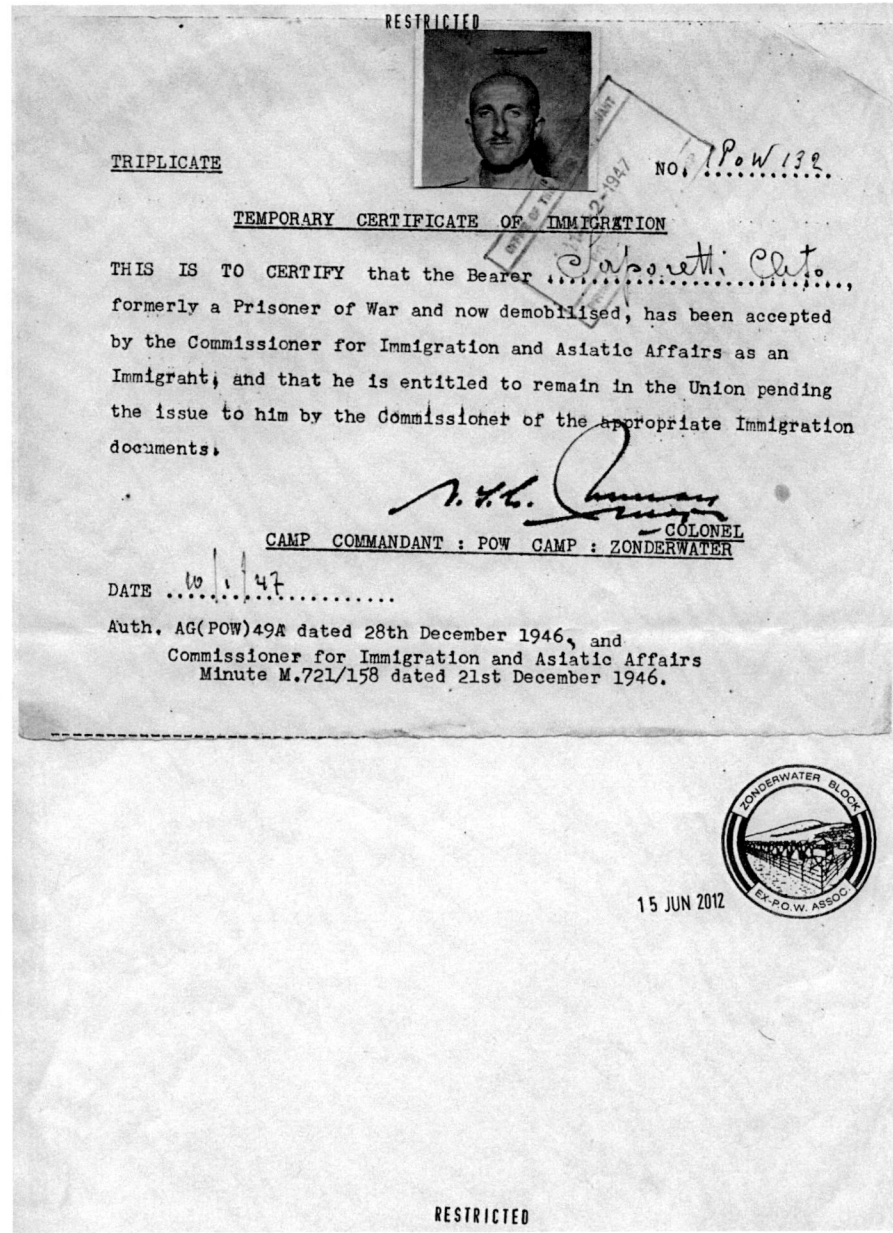

RESTRICTED

TRIPLICATE   NO. *PoW 132*

TEMPORARY CERTIFICATE OF IMMIGRATION

THIS IS TO CERTIFY that the Bearer *Saporetti Cht.*,
formerly a Prisoner of War and now demobilised, has been accepted
by the Commissioner for Immigration and Asiatic Affairs as an
Immigrant; and that he is entitled to remain in the Union pending
the issue to him by the Commissioner of the appropriate Immigration
documents.

COLONEL
CAMP COMMANDANT : POW CAMP : ZONDERWATER

DATE *10.1.47*

Auth. AG(POW)49A dated 28th December 1946, and
    Commissioner for Immigration and Asiatic Affairs
       Minute M.721/158 dated 21st December 1946.

15 JUN 2012

RESTRICTED

Saporetti, POW number 258419, is allowed to remain in South Africa after
his release from Zonderwater Camp.

Cleto's accommodation while on parole at Dundarach poultry farm, owned by Alistair Stuart, 1947.

Nine post-dated cheques which Cleto gave to Ben Godfrey in payment for Lemoenkloof Poultry Farm, Klipheuwel, Western Cape Province.

Willy de Villiers, Lemoenkloof farm manager and subsequent MD of Lemoenkloof Holdings, was a major reason for the company's success.

Lemoenkloof Poultry Farm, with its name changed to "Amaqanda Farms", 2012. At 220 hectares it accommodates 600,000 chickens and sells only eggs.

Cleto almost lost his life when he crashed his Oldsmobile on the farm road.

Cleto with wife Letty gazing at him fondly. His sister in law, Lara, is by his side.

Tokai CHIX lay the best eggs. After Newcastle Disease disaster, Lemoenkloof rises from the ashes. Willy de Villiers purchases chicks from Julian Mirvish.

Giuseppe Chisin, ex POW, with wife Paulina, lived and worked on Lemoenkloof for 30 years.

Orlando Valacchi, ex POW and former professional cyclist, hale and hearty at 92 years.

Giuseppe Caputo, whose father, Antonio, ex POW, lived on Lemoenkloof.

Ron Hobkirk, High Rustenberg farm manager for 30 years, and trustee of the Saporetti Foundation.

Graeme Dale Kuys, Cleto's long-time accountant and executor of the Saporetti Foundation.

Cleto before his lifestyle change.

Cleto, 20 kgs lighter after his change to a healthy diet, with his brother Carlo, the dentist.

Cleto was awarded the title of *Commendatore* by the Italian government, 1969.

Ernesto Partisani, Cleto's good friend in Forli, Italy.

Boris Chaitow, Chiropracter and Naturopath. Principal at the Hydro, 1972–1982. Trained at Champneys, UK, with uncle, Stanley Lief.

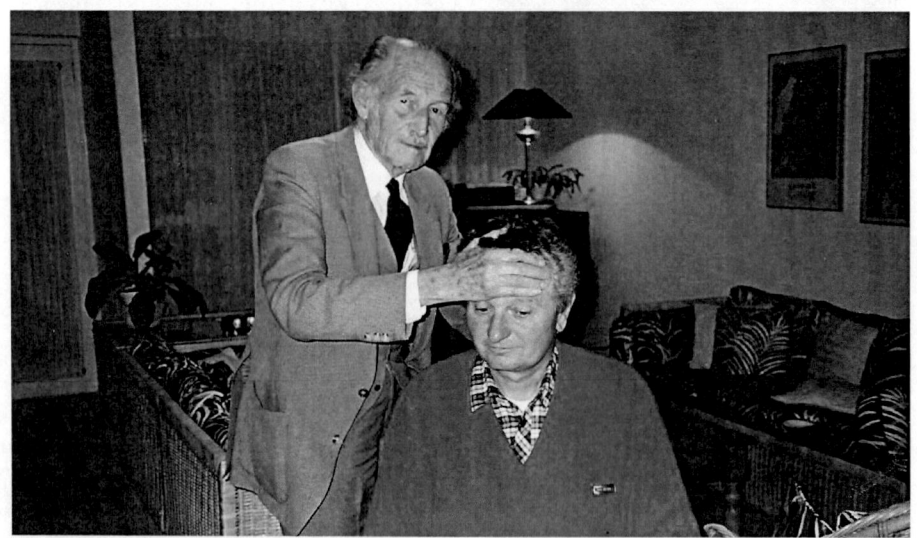

Boris Chaitow with Dante Vernetti in Cape Town.

Saporetti invites Chris Barnard to visit the Hydro.

"You are what you eat" – Cleto entertains guests at the Hydro with his breadmaking skills. His bread contained 28 ingredients.

Margaret Gardener, Miss South Africa, with shop manager Ella Steyn and Cleto.

Cleto welcomes "Infogate" politician Eschel Rhoodie and wife Katie to the Hydro.

Emiliano and Monica Sandri entertain Cleto and Theresa du Plessis at La Perla restaurant in Sea Point.

Cleto kept a Citroen Pallas in Italy for use during his frequent visits.

High Rustenberg Health Hydro, Ida's Valley, Stellenbosch – founded 1972.

The Hydro diet: three fruits per day, artfully displayed, with vegetable soup at 4 pm.

Kitchen staff under the expert eye of Anna Erlank created superb salads.

Rose was a true artist with her vegetable carvings.

The salad buffet on Wednesdays and Sundays was famous and attracted many visitors.

Fruit was always part of the Hydro regime.

Nurses Theresa, Debbie, Sharon, Tertia, Magda, and Esther, were all trained as lifestyle consultants practising Naturopathy. Ron Hobkirk, Anna Erlank and dietician Cornie Kirsten made up a wonderful team.

Geraldine Mitton lectures to Hydro guests and to the public on healthy lifestyle practices.

The new indoor pool, venue for popular Water Aerobics.

The Hydro was honoured by a visit from Nelson Mandela.

The Cleto Saporetti Foundation Mobile Nutrition Unit tackled farm roads over an area of 800 square kilometres in Stellenbosch.

Ron Hobkirk and Graeme Dale Kuys with a second Mobile Nutrition Unit.

Charlotte Okkers, Ansaaf Crombie and Johanna Kobo were popular nutrition educators.

Anna Erlank, Cornelia Kirsten and Ansaaf Crombie made sure that the Hydro was promoted at many Stellenbosch functions.

Business tycoon, Donald Gordon, joins participants at a stress management workshop led by Professor George Jaros.

Guests attending the Gala Opening of the new facilities in 1987 look forward to the salad buffet.

Chiropracter Juan van Breda and Natasha keep fit in the forest.

Tertia Schoeman with Dr Tim O'Moloney who survived after crashing his Rover at a railway crossing.

Ron Hobkirk with regular guest, Isabel Belinsky, cattle breeder from Zimbabwe, planted a tree every Arbour Day.

Ron Hobkirk and Boris Chaitow join Geraldine Mitton for an outing in Stellenbosch.

Pieter-Dirk Uys aka Evita Bezuidenhout enjoyed time to relax at the Hydro.

Tessa Uys, concert pianist, and sister of Pieter, entertained guests with her superb playing.

Former President Lucas Mangope and wife Leah invited Dr Mitton to his 70th birthday at Motswedi in 1993. A frequent guest at the Hydro, he kept fit in his impressive home gym.

Geraldine Mitton discovers that Naturopathy has much in common with Traditional Chinese Medicine at Shaanxi University, XIAN Peoples' Republic of China

Student Chefs with Principal Letitia Prinsloo from the Institute of Culinary Arts in Stellenbosch take part in a Salad-making competition.

The Research unit at the Hydro where Cornelia Kirsten demonstrates healthy snacks to a guest.

Hydro Princesses promote the Saporetti Foundation and the schools Health Fair in Stellenbosch.

Mr Muscles Competition at Lourensford Estate, Stellenbosch.

Joan Huskisson, Head of Dietetics at UCT Medical School, and members of the Nutrition Society, visit the Hydro.

Trustees Ron Hobkirk and Barry Loftus present a stove to a vegetable gardens winner, one of 500 entries, in Ido's Valley, Stellenbosch.

Vegetable Gardens Competition, 1996 – three winners with their splendid turnips.

Abraham November won 3rd prize for his vegetable garden.

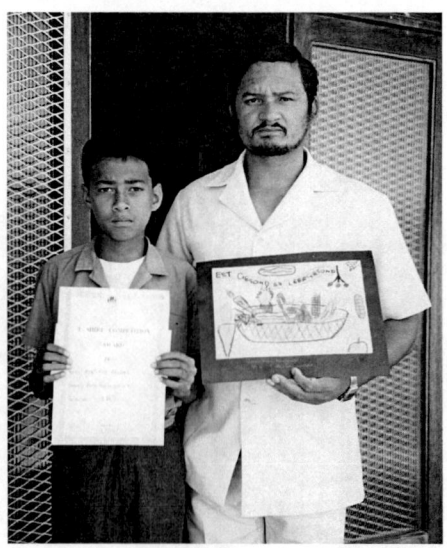

Teacher and pupil from Ida's Valley Primary, hold prize-winning entry in the Saporetti Foundation T-shirt competition with theme "Eet gesond".

Charlotte and Ansaaf give a nutrition demo at a clinic in Stellenbosch.

Dietician Cornelia Kirsten explains how health choices will make these youngsters soccer stars of the future.

Role play is always popular. Ansaaf, aka "Sannie", is coached by fellow nutrition educator, Charlotte.

The Saporetti Community Centre in Cloetesville, former Rastifarian hideout, was painted and decorated by Stellenbosch University students.

Volunteer women from Cloetesville assist with feeding and entertaining the youngsters. Salads and Hydro health bread are delivered daily.

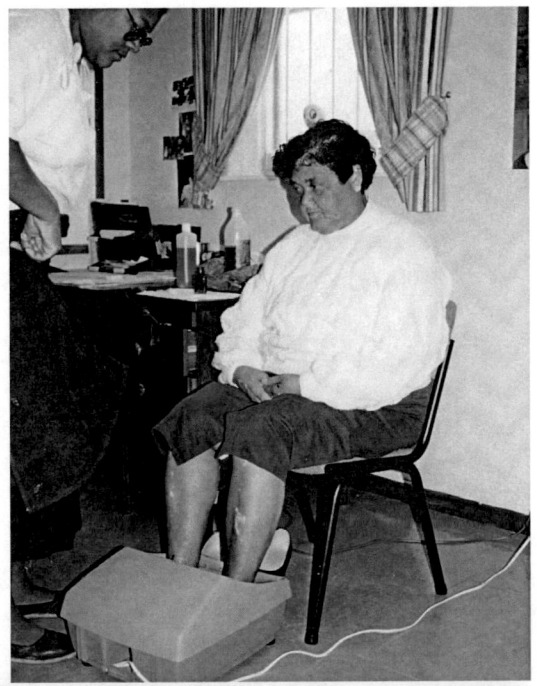

"My poor aching feet!" Mrs Cornelius at Ebenezer Old Age Home has some welcome relief. Nutrition educators regularly visit senior citizens, offer massages and promote physical exercise.

Stellenbosch "Drompoppies" (drum majorettes) from Ebenezer Old Age Home are full of energy during a parade.

Senior citizens Picnic and Health Day organised by the Saporetti Foundation.

Sports Day: Senior Citizens coached by the nutrition educators won 1st prize.

Over 6,000 excited primary school children attended the Health Fair held at Cloetesville Secondary School in Stellenbosch.

Peter Langeveldt Primary School took part in the Schools Health Fair, 1993.

The Stellenbosch Traffic Department demonstrated road rules and safety.

This school warns against the use of drugs at the Schools' Health Fair.

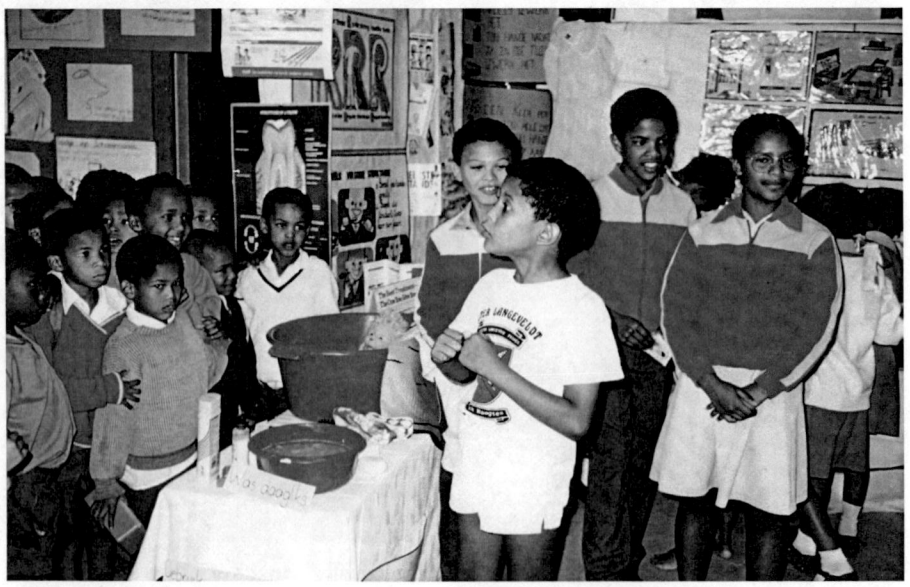

An enthusiastic learner demonstrates hygiene in the home.

"Mommie! Pappie! Is jy lief vir my? Eet gesond en leef goed. Ek het jou nodig." "Mother! Father! Do you love me? Eat healthily and live properly. I need you."

Saporetti Foundation Trustees Barry Loftus and Ron Hobkirk meet Stellenbosch Mayor at the Health Fair.

THE HYDRO
1971–1984

A wise man ought to realise that his health
is his most valuable possession
(Hippocrates)

There is a saying that when one door closes another one opens. In this case the open door led to High Rustenburg Estate in Stellenbosch, which fortuitously became available in 1971. Cleto had sold Lemoenkloof but still retained 50% together with Letty in the Lemoenkloof Holding Company. He was no longer *Il Padrone*, required in the day to day running of the poultry farm which was now in the capable hands of Willy de Villiers.

With his conversion to a healthy lifestyle, especially after reading Luigi Carnaro's philosophy on diet and after meeting Boris Chaitow, Cleto was determined to establish a health farm in South Africa devoted to what was known at that time as Nature Cure.

Cleto had been searching for the ideal site for a health farm. He required a suitable environment and an existing house and buildings which could be developed. After meeting Chaitow in the U.K., Cleto invited him to visit Cape Town in 1969 to assist with the search, but his visit did not provide any viable propositions and he returned to the U.K.

Aubrey Weston had purchased High Rustenburg Estate from the dowager Lady de Villiers, and had built a comfortable house on the property. The farm of 38 hectares was situated on the mountainside overlooking the stunningly beautiful Ida's Valley on the outskirts of Stellenbosch. Some years previously, Aubrey had been in the South African army combined with the British forces which had captured Cleto in Eritrea. Weston owned a paint factory in Cape Town which he sold at a handsome profit. He was paid in part by shares which were worth R75 at the time. Aubrey decided to celebrate and left with a number of his friends for an extended and lavish holiday in the south of France. Champagne flowed, and the Negresco luxury hotel in Nice provided them with a glamorous venue for their boisterous parties. Returning after three months he was horrified to find that his shares were now worth only R7,50.

High Rustenburg had been left in the capable hands of his farm manager, Ron Hobkirk. Ron was instructed to sell High Rustenburg and negotiated the sale with an excited Saporetti who paid R270,000 for the property. Aubrey Weston never returned to Stellenbosch and was last heard of in Zimbabwe. Ron Hobkirk stayed on as Cleto's trusted right-hand man and became a trustee after Cleto's death in 1984. Ron was to remain on the farm for over 30 years until it was sold by the trustees in 2002.

Cleto sent a cable to Boris Chaitow after the purchase stating: "Bought High Rustenburg Estate. We can operate any time."

Prior to his purchase of High Rustenburg, Cleto had been very active in his attempts to persuade the Department of Health, insurance companies, the Medical Association, and even South Africa's tobacco giants, to promote health and to help prevent chronic disease. He considered that this would be achieved by following a healthy, calorie-restricted diet, physical exercise, and the implementation of stress-coping strategies. "We are what we eat, drink, breathe and think!"

His booklet *Memorandum of Health* was passionate, but seriously longwinded and written in terminology which was not enticing for the health professionals to whom it was directed. He did not endear himself to the tobacco companies by quoting the words of Dr Frank Mitchell, former Medical Officer of Health, who had bravely asserted: "Cigarette smoking is a socially acceptable method of suicide".

In response to his letters to the above-mentioned organisations, Cleto received only discouraging replies, including the following:

> *"We regret that further dialogue on a non-specific level will be to no avail and smoking and health will only be resolved by basic scientific research."*

Cleto was not discouraged, and pressed on with his endeavours.

> *"Health is of no less importance than wealth. Why not apply business principles to our health, and implement annual stock-taking? Are we doing everything in our power to conserve health? Are we using our physical machines in such a way that they will wear out before their time?"*

Cleto recommended seven foundation stones on which to build health: a good diet; water; sunshine; exercise; rest; fresh air; and mental health.

After writing a lengthy letter to a leading insurance company suggesting that they promote preventive health through their organisation, he was surprised when he was asked to meet their M.D., the chairman, and four medical doctors. They were polite, but no action was taken. At this meeting he shared his vision regarding the establishment of a health resort. He also told them of his intention that health education should be available to the underprivileged.

His dietary advice, written in 1970, is valid today. He advocated the avoidance of refined carbohydrates, sugar, soft drinks, processed foods and saturated fats, He emphasised the focus on fruit, vegetables, grains and nuts, together with fish and lean meat. A few years later, when the Hydro had been operating for several years, Cleto wrote another booklet *The Natural Way to Health* where he recommended a restricted diet or controlled fasting as a way to give the body a rest and 'house cleaning'.

In those days, Cleto was regarded as 'freaky' by many of the medical profession, including those who frequented his restaurants. He subsequently invited many of them to visit the Hydro. Government and parliamentary officials were invited. Were they impressed? Did they change their habits and lifestyle? Did they acknowledge the increase in wellbeing and vitality after a week to 10 days of complimentary health care? They certainly enjoyed the wonderful surroundings of High Rustenburg but few, if any, were convinced of the philosophy.

Cleto was passionate about Nature Cure but he was no orator, and he was also limited by his suboptimal command of English. However, Boris Chaitow was, from the outset, a dynamic and charismatic speaker. His lectures were legendary. He converted many thousands of Hydro guests who still, today, talk about his influence.

Boris Chaitow was 64-years-old when he came to the Hydro. At an age when many men were retiring, Boris applied energy and passion to fulfilling Cleto's dream. Born in Latvia in 1907, he came to South Africa at a young age and, after qualifying as a lawyer and working for a few years, left for the US to study further, this time in chiropractic.

His cousin, Stanley Lief, 15 years his senior, was the foremost naturopath in the UK. He too had emigrated with his family from Latvia to South Africa. Years later he took over Champneys which became the first natural health retreat in England. Apart from expanding the philosophy of Nature Cure, he developed a specific neuromuscular technique involving soft tissue manipulation, still highly regarded today and strongly supported by Boris's nephew, Leon Chaitow, a well-known naturopath, osteopath and acclaimed author of more than 40 books.

Lief sponsored Boris's education in the US and in return Boris worked as his associate at Champneys for several years. Lief was a charismatic personality and a strict disciplinarian. His character and adherence to the principles of naturopathy were clearly adopted by Boris who brought these characteristics to his 10 years of directing operations at the Hydro. Lief was a pioneering naturopath and his work is continued through the school he helped to establish, the doctors he trained, and the public who were educated in the principles of Nature Cure.

After many career moves, Chaitow took up a position as Director of Therapeutics at Enton Hall in the U.K. It was here that Cleto initially met Boris and told him of his dream to open a health resort in South Africa. When Cleto purchased High Rustenburg Estate, he asked Boris to relocate and to commence operations.

The Hydro opened its doors in January 1972 as a Natural Healing resort with the emphasis on controlled fasting, mainly raw foods, exercise, relaxation, sunshine, fresh air, and an "atmosphere of dedicated service".

Using the Champneys' model, Boris took charge. Starting with only three rooms, he trained staff and implemented a strict regime for guests to follow. Boris called them patients. Controlled fasting and a mainly raw food vegetarian diet was the catalyst whereby healing took place. Every guest had a daily massage, hydrotherapy and osteopathic manipulation. Colonic irrigation, known as the 'Royal Flush', was given twice-weekly to 'eliminate toxins'.

Nature Cure philosophy states that every person has the ability to heal himself or herself, if given the environment to do so. Correct nutrition is the cornerstone, and holistic treatments include fasting, massage, hydrotherapy, relaxation, and muscle manipulation.

Chaitow implemented his programmes without concession. He applied them with strong discipline and he had total confidence in his work. His lectures left patients feeling like sinful transgressors. Standing at his podium in full cry, he kept a bucket by his side and asked the audience to imagine throwing all the food and drink consumed each day into it. His audience, weak and feeble through lack of food and suffering nausea, headaches and muscle pains due to caffeine withdrawal, were suitably chastised and promised to mend their ways. They left the Hydro kilos lighter, energised and revitalised, converted to Rooibos tea and promising to keep Mondays as 'fruit only' days. Boris inspired thousands of guests who experienced a sense of wellbeing which encouraged them to book in to the Hydro for their annual 'Spring Clean'.

Of course, the fact that they lost weight was a strong incentive. The Hydro became known as the 'Fat Farm', a term used by derogatory non-Hydro-goers and especially the medical profession.

In those days, the Royal Flush was administered twice weekly by Sister Patience, who proudly announced that she had delivered 5,600 babies in her former career. The aim was to rid the colon of all the accumulated and compacted waste.

Guests felt cleansed both physically and emotionally after their sessions, administered with great empathy by Sister Patience, who in addition to her other skills was a talented poet. Apart from the benefit of weight loss, the newly gained 'flat tummy' motivated the recipients to kick-start their new health regime. However, medical doctors, especially gastroenterologists, condemned colon hydrotherapy which they regarded as being dangerous and referred to the Hydro as "that place where they feed you lettuce leaves and give you enemas".

HIGH RUSTENBERG HYDRO
By Sister Irene Patience

Up yonder hill the Hydro hidden
With lustrous valley and fruit forbidden
Apples rosy and sweet, yet Adam forbids while Eve cleaves to the fig
Vines, the Kelsey plums, Stein Grapes, Boncretian pears
Roses red, strelitzias yellow and blue gum trees attract the busy bee.
Lofty mountains: Simonsberg with Table Mountain in the distance
Vivid to the naked eye.
Global foreigners by land, sea, sky, keep the pace with a smile.
Celestial bodies sweep across the sky
while Nimbus, Stratus Cirrus and Cumulus clouds
change the starry heaven from time to time.
The golden moon in its full phase welcomes wearied
sojourners who seek refuge at the Haven
with high hopes in a foreign land, and then
follow the mad band of starvation with
Innovation and Motivation.
Yes, indeed – what fools would chance to enhance
the future furthermore of nature.
Setbacks, despair, immortality, sex control, lust,
bodily harm over indulgence; cures the mind body and soul.
At last they have reached their goal.
Rejuvenated, inspirited yet reluctant of their sin
Yes tomorrow Oh! Tomorrow brings us to our goal.
Not through toil and strife comes the Hydro's call
for aim and refrain.

In 1972, the original three treatment rooms were extended to include the first 14 accommodation rooms in the West wing. A small staff complement was trained by Chaitow. He consulted the guests on arrival and insisted on daily chiropractic treatments. His wife, Madeleine, a talented artist, supervised the kitchen and attended to the furnishing and décor. The only road leading up to the Hydro was a gravel path in very bad condition. The farm tractor was on constant standby to rescue cars from the mud.

In 1975, one of the curtains in Chaitow's office caught fire from a wall heater, destroying the entire front of the building. After rebuilding, construction operations continued each year with an East wing and an enlarged West wing which provided bedrooms and some inexpensive cottages and mobiles units until, by 1988, over 100 guests could be accommodated.

In spite of, or because of the strict regime, guests generally emerged from the Hydro feeling revitalised, alert and healthy. Blood pressure normalised, aches and pains vanished, digestive problems subsided and diabetic patients found that their blood sugar levels returned to normal. Guests who arrived stressed and irritable returned home with a new sense of wellbeing. Insomniacs were able to sleep peacefully. Tasting food became a new experience. Some guests even managed to quit smoking. Which pharmaceutical medications could achieve the same results?

Guests were so enthusiastic that they returned annually for the detox and spring clean. It was likened to taking one's car in for a service. With the Hydro's fame spreading by word of mouth, guests arrived from all over South Africa, Namibia, Mauritius, the rest of

Africa, and up to 18 per cent came from overseas, mostly the UK and Germany.

In the early days Cleto often stood quietly near the reception area when guests arrived. One elegant lady mistook him for a porter and ordered him to take her bags to her room. He politely complied and accepted the 20 cents tip.

Renata Vernetti was one of the guests during those early days. Cleto hopped past her, with a plaster of Paris cast covering his left foot and ankle. *"Eco! Look how healthy I am!"* Cleto demonstrated this by doing a somersault in the lounge. Quite remarkable considering that he had fractured 27 bones in his car accident some years previously. Cleto was now 68-years-old.

Renata survived on a single orange for breakfast, an apple for lunch and another orange for supper. Vegetable soup at 4 pm was the highlight of the day with all the guests gathering to discuss their symptoms. Some desperate guests offered substantial bribes to purchase extra fruit. One of the large ladies, the wife of a cabinet minister, ventured out into the orchards looking for some form of edible sustenance. The assistant farm manager, thinking that he saw a thief, let off a warning blast from his shotgun.

Fasting was too difficult for some guests who ended up sneaking into Stellenbosch searching for food. *Mamma Roma* was the preferred Italian restaurant with a regular Hydro clientele. When housekeeping cleaned the rooms after departure, empty whiskey bottles were occasionally found on the tops of cupboards.

In the seventies, antioxidants had not yet been recognised. The terms 'antioxidants' and 'free radicals' only became buzz words in the nineties. Today we all know that fruit and vegetables provide a variety of antioxidants and vitamins which are so essential in the prevention of disease. Calorie restriction has been shown to enhance longevity. At overseas clinics such as the Buchinger in Germany, controlled fasting is known as 'intestinal resting' and is practised for two to three weeks.

But back then the medical profession in South Africa was dubious about the Hydro diet of fruit and raw vegetables. "What about sufficient protein?", they cried. Abstaining from meat and fish, as well as caffeine and alcohol, for a week or ten days, created a definite state of well-being.

Sisters Veronica and Eleanor Hendricks were the earliest employees at the Hydro, remaining a loyal and hardworking part of the Hydro family for 25 years. Returning guests regarded them as special friends. Annual visitor John Donner, an ex-Cold Stream guard who stood 1.95 metres tall in his socks, found it difficult to exist on the semi-fast. After suffering for a week he was rewarded with excellent chicken curry at the Hendricks' home in Ida's Valley. Sister Patience always baked him a fruit cake to take home to the UK when he left.

Veronica recalls that when the Hydro opened its doors in January 1972 there were only four guests. Eleanor knew how to reassure apprehensive arrivals who were ready to leave when they heard about the 'diet'. Guests from Namibia were a particular problem. Meat eaters and serial coffee drinkers, they nevertheless loved the lush greenery, orchards and forest which made the environment so appealing. Most of the guests did not know that Cleto was the owner until Eleanor pointed him out.

Cleto and Letty entertained the guests with bread-making demos, Cleto demonstrating his amazing bread which contained 28 different ingredients. There were regular fashion shows with guests acting as models. Ella Steyn was the shop manager and did a roaring trade disposing of her wares after these fashion parades. At these functions, Cleto, dressed in a blonde wig and wearing gown and slippers, ended the show by racing around the swimming pool on a small motor bike, then falling into the water.

Farm manager Ron Hobkirk described Cleto's method of tackling expansion: "I am spending R100,000 on extensions this year and I want you to help me to see that we are all ready to open in January next year".

"R100,000 in 1971 was a large sum of money to risk on an unknown venture," remarked Ron, "but I realised that with Cleto's drive and determination it was bound to be a success".

It took less than six months to build the West wing, massage rooms, and hydrotherapy unit with separate facilities for males and females.

The recommended stay at the Hydro was 10–14 days in order to obtain the maximum benefit of the cleansing diet together with the daily therapies. The therapeutic staff included five chiropractors and one naturopath, thus guests had personal attention during their stay. Guests were monitored every second day, and their weight loss was keenly anticipated. Woe betide if they had not lost kilos in spite of existing on three fruits a day. Of course there were those who cheated with snacks and biltong smuggled in their suitcases.

The kitchen staff created superb salads with artistic vegetable carvings. The buffets on Wednesdays and Sundays were famous. Every guest looked forward to their daily massage with their own dedicated masseur. The 20 masseurs were the best in the country and were transported daily from their homes in Ida's Valley. During the restricted diet, the only exercise prescribed was gentle walking on the farm, although yoga and progressive relaxation classes were available to those who wanted them.

Cleto's relationship with Chaitow was stormy. Ron Hobkirk and staff often heard shouting. It was unusual for Cleto to have difficult business relationships, but their differences were probably related to financial matters. Cleto was continuing to invest large sums into the running of the Hydro and he no doubt felt that some of the demands were unreasonable. After one such altercation, Cleto was heard to say "I closed him the mouth!"

On one occasion, Cleto arrived back from one of his frequent trips to Italy and found a portrait of Boris hanging in the reception area. Beneath it was a plaque with the words "Dr Boris Chaitow. Founder of The Hydro". The portrait was removed forthwith.

In 1982, Chaitow was advised by cardiac surgeon, Dr Marius Barnard, that he needed cardiac surgery. Boris refused, maintaining that he would rather have treatment in the UK.

Telling staff at the Hydro that he and Madeleine were going on holiday, Boris relocated to the UK where he purchased his nephew Leon Chaitow's house and practice in Worthing, Sussex. Leon then moved abroad. The year was 1982. Boris had been at the Hydro for 10 years.

Boris then flew to Italy where Cleto was resting, having recently been diagnosed with bladder cancer. We are told that Boris made a number of excessive financial demands which enraged Cleto. "He held a knife to my throat", recalled Cleto who ordered Chaitow to never set foot in the Hydro again.

Saporetti flew back to South Africa and informed the staff at the Hydro that Boris would not be returning. There were already four chiropractors, Doctors Chadwick, Roberts, Schonfeldt, and Melville, and naturopath Dr Dowling on the staff. In addition, Cleto appointed Dr Briggs (also a chiropractor) overall in charge.

In a letter to the guests Cleto, in his role as founder, announced:

> *"I thought that you would like to know a little more about the founder of High Rustenburg Hydro. I am a South African of Italian origin and have lived in your beautiful country for the past 35 years.*
>
> *I must add that I am a widower with no children. This fact has some bearing on what I am about to say.*
>
> *Some 12 years ago, I established the first centre of natural healing of its kind in South Africa. It has since then achieved fame and success beyond all my expectations, not due to the objective of financial gain, but because of dedication to the simple philosophy of health living.*
>
> *The Hydro has cost several million rands to bring into being.*
>
> *I do not require financial assistance to ensure its perpetuity.*
>
> *It is your support that will ensure the Hydro's continuance for posterity".*

On the occasion of the Hydro's first annual staff party, held at the Van der Stel Club in Stellenbosch, on 25th February 1983, 120 staff members were present. Cleto welcomed them all and spoke of the current status of the Hydro. He assured them that he was still as involved, dedicated and enthusiastic as he had been on the first day when he and Dr Chaitow had opened the doors with only three rooms, and stated:

> "It was reported in the media that my role was purely that of a backer, the man who put up the money, but this was not accurate. Apart from my very real commitment to the philosophy of the Hydro, I offered some 60 years of modest business experience and a great deal of hard work.
>
> I ask you to join me in wishing Dr and Mrs Chaitow good health and happiness and every success in their new venture in England.
>
> If everything goes according to my wishes, the Hydro will one day be administered as a trust for the benefit of all, in the years to come. It is true we still encounter prejudice which is the result of ignorance, but in the not too distant future our efforts will be more widely understood by the open minded and the informed. In time, large institutions and government bodies dealing with health will appreciate more fully our endeavours to the greater benefit of society at large".

After his fall out with Cleto, Boris returned to the UK. A short while later he had a heart attack while out walking and was admitted to Worthing Hospital. His stepson, Brian Wilson, also a chiropractor, assisted by taking over the practice and supporting his mother.

One year later, in 1984, Cleto died in Cape Town. After Cleto's death, Boris contacted Ron Hobkirk, now a trustee as well as the farm manager, and asked if he could return to the Hydro. Ron agreed to provide Boris and Madeleine with a cottage, all meals and other requirements. Thus Boris returned at the age of 79. However, his restlessness continued and it wasn't long before he packed a container with all their possessions and his car to travel all the way to New Zealand to stay with Madeleine's son Brian, who had opened his practice in Papakura.

After a short while, Boris and Madeleine returned to the Hydro where Madeleine passed away in 1988. Still restless, Boris then travelled to the US where he stayed with a former patient for several months after which he returned to the Hydro and remained there until his death in 1995. Although he was lonely without Madeleine, the Hydro staff were caring and spent time with him each day. His three sons from his first marriage live in the UK.

Boris Chaitow's work and influence at the Hydro lasted for ten years, from 1972 until 1982.

Was the Hydro unique? It certainly was the first health farm in South Africa devoted to what was known at the time as Nature Cure. Similar establishments included Champneys in the UK, on which Boris based his philosophy. The Buchinger fasting clinics in Uberlingen and Marbella were, and still are, headed by family generations of medical doctors. In Austria, the Mayr Clinic used stale bread rolls in their semi fasting regime. Today, of course, a new generation and new variety of destination health resorts has arisen worldwide.

Many of the guests from Germany, Switzerland and Austria who visited the Hydro were accustomed to the regime of fasting. There was a bonus for travelling to South Africa for their annual Detox and

Cleanse. Including airfare, the cost was far less than similar resorts in Europe. Moreover, the glorious weather and superb scenery, together with a friendly and professional staff, made returning guests feel part of the Hydro family. Many guests booked a year ahead, and made sure that they would be there together with the same friends.

THE ESTATE, THE FOUNDATION,
AND DRAMA IN ITALY
1984

Look to your health; and if you have it
praise God and value it next to a good conscience.
For health is the second blessing that we mortals
are capable of; a blessing that money cannot buy.
(Izaak Walton 1593–1683)

During the 1970s Saporetti started formulating his idea of leaving his estate to finance his dream of healthier people in South Africa. He had long discussions with his accountant and future executor, Graeme Dale Kuys. With the advice of Advocate Meyerowitz, the Saporetti Foundation was accepted as a charitable trust by the Secretary for Inland Revenue, thus freeing the estate from estate duty.

During his many visits to his home town of Ravenna, and visits to his properties in Riccione, Monte Fiore, Porto Verde and Naples, Cleto met with his good friend Ernesto Partisani and asked his own lawyer, Aldo Barzanti, to draw up a will for all his assets in Italy. Cleto informed Dale Kuys, Ron Hobkirk, and also Partisani and Barzanti, that it was his intention to create another 'High Rustenburg Hydro' in Italy. In those days there were many Italian spas and resorts with mineral baths and *Fango* (mud baths), but they did not promote diet or fasting. In fact, it would have been a huge task to persuade Italians to forego their pasta, *prosciutto* and espressos in exchange for an apple three times a day, hot water and lemon, and some insipid vegetable broth. However, with Cleto's enthusiasm and drive, one could be certainly assured of success.

Establishment of the Italian Hydro was to be achieved by selling eight properties in Italy, in addition to liquid assets held by Barzanti. When discussing his Italian will, Cleto reportedly told his friends and advisors that his two brothers, Walter and Carlo, were sufficiently well off and did not require financial assistance. The Saporetti family home in Via Alfredo Baccarini, Ravenna, was to remain with his nephew Leonardo Senni. Cleto's grandparents and parents had lived there since the early 1900s and the fourth generation of Saporettis were presently residing there.

Saporetti's South African will was signed on May 30th, 1984. He died a month later, on June 20th 1984, at the age of 79, in his Sea Point apartment. He had been cared for by his nurse Ansie van Wyk and attended by Theresa du Plessis, his loyal companion, for the past seven years. After a service at the Catholic Church in Sea Point, he was cremated according to his wishes.

Six days before his death, the Italian will was nowhere to be found, and thus a second Italian will was drawn up, which was brought to him in his Cape Town apartment, and which he signed on June 14th. In this will he left his properties in Italy to members of his family and friends in Italy, and any mention of an Italian Hydro was absent. It was thought that he had changed his mind regarding his Italian assets.

The South African executors contested the second Italian will on the grounds that Saporetti was gravely ill and not able to think clearly at the time the will was signed. An advocate was sent to Italy who conferred with a senior lawyer in Rome. The result was that the second will was recognised and all of the Italian properties were bequeathed to family members.

Cleto's dream of establishing a health clinic in Italy was never realised.

This was truly unfortunate. Apart from his passion to introduce healthy lifestyle practices to that country, as an Italian without heirs he would have wanted to leave a legacy in his native land.

Saporetti realised that the Hydro would gain credibility and greater recognition if it were headed by a medical doctor as principal. This had been discussed with Dale Kuys and others for at least four years before Cleto's death. During 1983 he sent a letter to the South African Medical and Dental Council requesting permission to appoint a medical doctor.

"Honourable sirs,

Nine years ago, imbued by my own and many other people's experience, and determined that I owed it to mankind to spread the gospel as to how I was restored to perfect health and vitality after many years as a chronic invalid I decided to open a Nature Cure Resort which is now the famous High Rustenburg Hydro.

The response was phenomenal and the success beyond all my expectations, although not necessarily financially, but as a wealthy man I have accepted the fact that my duty to mankind is more important than financial gain.

I am now 78 years of age and my greatest concern at the moment is to establish perpetuity in the event of my demise. The Hydro at this point in time is run by a team of very capable men all experts in their own field as Chiropractors, Osteopaths and Naturopaths but none of them have a medical degree and from time to time we have sensed a certain amount of resistance from the medical profession. It is this factor that has prompted me to write to you.

I too feel that the time has come when the Principal of the Hydro should be a medical doctor, for a person of that background could only enhance what we are trying to achieve. Unfortunately I understand that under the present regulations they are prevented from accepting such a position.

Whilst not questioning this regulation I would respectfully suggest that it would only serve to improve our service to mankind if we had a medically trained Principal to direct our operations.

Our doors are open at all times to anyone wishing to come and see what we are doing. The satisfied and rejuvenated patients that have by the thousand passed through these doors, are testimony enough of what we have achieved.

I wait with interest your kind consideration of my request.

Yours sincerely,

Cleto Saporetti

Cleto's request fell on deaf ears. At that time it was taboo for a medical doctor to work in association with chiropractors. One wonders whether Cleto had discussed this with Boris Chaitow and if this was one of the reasons that had contributed to his departure in 1982. We know that he had heart problems and had refused to have treatment in South Africa. Ron Hobkirk, trustee and resident on the farm, was told by Boris that he was going on holiday only.

Saporetti's will covering his South African assets was divided into two trusts, the Saporetti Family Trust, with bequests to family members and friends, and the Cleto Saporetti Foundation, of which High Rustenburg Hydro formed a part.

> *"The object of the Foundation shall be research into and study of Nature Cure, with diet being of great importance; the teaching and practice thereof and in general the propagation of the philosophy and practice of Nature Cure. I believe that these objects will be in the interest of the people of South Africa leading to higher standards of health and wellbeing."*

Cleto instructed that the finances of the foundation be utilised for the following:

- Establishment of a chair at a university or alternately the establishment of a research unit to study and disseminate knowledge relating to Nature Cure.
- Establishment of clinics devoted to the practice of Nature Cure, and to provide financial assistance to the less privileged.
- Establishment of a Senior Citizens' home.

The term Nature Cure later became known as Naturopathy and incorporated into the principles of a healthy lifestyle.

It was remarkable that Cleto documented his desire to promote Nature Cure at a time when the medical profession and medical bodies were totally against any form of what they considered to be Alternative Medicine. It was later called Complementary Medicine. He was totally convinced, due mainly to the benefits he himself had experienced after his near-fatal car accident in 1955. He had also witnessed improvements in his poultry when they were fed the correct nutrients. Nowadays, a vegetarian diet, calorie restriction, hydrotherapy and relaxation therapies are mainstream and can hardly be called 'alternative'. Today there is a university course in Naturopathy but this only came about two decades after Saporetti's death.

In the years prior to his death, Cleto and Graeme Dale Kuys had numerous discussions as to how to implement his wishes, bearing in mind the negative response from the medical bodies. By the time Cleto died they had still not reached a conclusion. Dale Kuys spent many months talking to various people until the idea crystallised that there should be a post of Foundation Director. He was not discouraged by the lack of enthusiasm from the Medical Council and he formulated a profile and job description for the Foundation Director, as follows:

- The Foundation Director should be a registered medical practitioner orientated to the philosophy of Nature Cure and holistic medicine.
- The Foundation Director will act as medical officer in charge at the Hydro and will utilise health facts and statistics therefrom for research purposes.
- The Foundation Director will do international research regarding Nature Cure and holistic medicine and their benefits, and disseminate the information to the South African public.

- The Foundation Director will create liaison with the Medical Association of SA, and the SA Medical and Dental Council to promote dialogue and to encourage acceptance of Complementary medicine.
- The Foundation Director will have ongoing liaison with universities and tertiary education facilities.
- In due course the Foundation Director will advise on the establishment of a Senior Citizens' home and other clinics.

Saporetti's desire to establish a chair in Naturopathy at a university was premature as it was not thought acceptable in 1986.

Meanwhile, to tackle the knotty problem of a medical doctor at the Hydro, Professor S.A. Strauss, Professor of Law and Advocate of the Supreme Court, was invited to visit the Hydro to have a general inspection of its activities and services. Professor Strauss provided the following advice:

- The SA Medical and Dental Council prevents collaboration between a medical practitioner and alternative practitioners, such as homeopaths and chiropractors, and states that it is prohibited.
- The SA Medical and Dental Council has ruled that it is undesirable for a medical practitioner to act as medical advisor to a health farm.
- If the Hydro advertises it facilities, this could be seen as indirect advertising for the doctor.
- There should be no objection to the position of Foundation Director, and as such making use of research material from alternative professionals.

- The Foundation Director should at all times be cautious in talking to the public, and should not be identified by name in any radio or TV programmes.

Geraldine Mitton's story

"This was the challenge I faced after accepting Graeme Dale Kuys' offer.

It was risky leaving the secure environment of Groote Schuur Hospital. My colleagues were really dubious. 'You're going to that freaky place where they feed you lettuce leaves?' was the incredulous response 'and what about those Crick-Crack chiropractors?'".

During the seven years of demanding and often exhausting work in a department which saw up to 50,000 patients each year, I felt that many emergencies and exacerbated chronic conditions could have been prevented. Strokes, heart attacks, diabetic complications and lung disease were but a few examples of preventable conditions. There were many patients who suffered from side effects of the multiple medications which had been prescribed by different doctors attending to them. I knew that preventive medicine and health promotion was the way to go.

Thus when Graeme Dale Kuys arrived on my doorstep, I was ready to take up the challenge and implement the wonderful and totally unique position and pioneering work as Saporetti Foundation Director."

A NEW ERA AT THE HYDRO
1986−2000

*The doctor of the future will give no medicine, but
will interest his patients in the care of the human frame
and in the cause and prevention of disease.*
(Thomas Edison)

A new era had begun at the Hydro. During the next decade, there was a gradual move to incorporate and integrate complementary therapies together with modern medical diagnostics into the practice of Nature Cure. The original philosophy was maintained and Geraldine Mitton had many discussions with Boris Chaitow who was now living at the Hydro, in retirement.

Therapies such as chiropractic, homeopathy, acupuncture, and reflexology were regarded as alternative and were strongly criticised and scorned by the medical profession. Over the years, alternative or complementary therapies became accepted and sought after by the public who were gradually realising that prescription drugs were not the answer to their chronic problems and minor ailments. In those early days, the use of vitamin and mineral supplements was regarded as unnecessary. Herbal and plant-based supplements were regarded as dangerous and homeopathic remedies were useless.

The path between orthodox medicine and so-called alternative medicine had to be trodden carefully. The South African Medical and Dental Council had very rigid ideas. Professor S.A. Strauss had advised Dr Mitton to keep a low profile. The strict fruit fast, colonic irrigation and chiropractic were regarded as dangerous. From cautious beginnings, leading members of the medical profession were invited to functions where they enjoyed non-threatening salad lunches, and a few brave ones even spent a few days or a week at the Hydro.

The original regime was continued. However it was soon realised that excellent outcomes could be achieved by increasing the portions of fruit given during the first couple of days. Originally, only one fruit for each meal was artfully presented to look quite substantial, making a total of three apples or oranges a day. Portions of fruit were increased and guests did not suffer major hunger pangs, but still experienced the benefits of a cleansing diet. Salads were introduced on day three with the gradual addition of cottage cheese, whole wheat bread and a baked potato. The baked potatoes were absolutely the best anyone had ever tasted! They were slow baked with crispy skins and soft interiors. Added cottage cheese made it a sublime experience. One of the female guests was heard to announce: "I have yet to meet a man who excites me more than this baked potato!"

It was noted that blood pressures normalised whilst diabetic guests showed dramatic improvement in their blood sugar levels. Guests who had digestive problems, food intolerance, leaky guts, irritable bowels, peptic ulcers and yeast overgrowth were all placed on modified diets and closely monitored. It helped that the resident dietician, Cornelia Kirsten, was able to advise, while the team as a whole explored the new field of nutritional medicine.

Guests were asked to reduce their caffeine intake before arrival but very few took heed of the warnings. Thus the sister's office was kept very busy on Mondays and Tuesdays. Queues of groaning patients with splitting headaches, nausea and muscular pains were miraculously relieved by 'Regmaak Remedy'. Ingredients remain a secret but included homeopathic magnesium sulphate which is excellent for muscle cramps. Sister Paddy Nagel, who had formerly instilled terror into junior nurses in the Paediatric wards at Groote Schuur Hospital, dished out her 'Stop Smoking Remedy'. A total of six prunes, to be sucked slowly through the day, really worked. Perhaps her smokers were equally terrified, but she had an almost 100 per cent success rate. Only homeopathic remedies were prescribed for coughs and colds, insomnia, and other ailments. The placebo effect was well recognised.

Cleto's bread-making demonstrations were replaced by salad-making demos which proved equally popular. However, the Hydro chef could not equal the flamboyance and hilarity created by Saporetti in his oversized chef's hat portraying the words, "You are what you eat".

At the end of each salad demo there would be a rush towards the buffet table to snatch a carrot, a celery stick, or some edible morsel to assuage hunger pains. Sufferers were soothed and consoled. "Don't worry. Just hang in there, you'll feel fantastic after a week!" Some guests even offered to sell their apples to the highest bidder, and some ravenous inmates chewed on their orange peels. Around the pool, the main topic of conversation was FOOD.

The spectacular salad buffets attracted many visitors on Wednesdays and Sundays, acting as a grand finale for those departing guests and a showcase to attract future clients to the Hydro.

Cornelia Kirsten printed a series of fact sheets which were given to guests to take home. Vitamins, minerals, specific foods for individual health problems, foods for diabetes, rheumatism, gout, heart disease and high blood pressure, were just some of the topics covered. Food combining, acid and alkaline foods were explained. She also designed a colourful new Food Guide Pyramid which clearly demonstrated healthy food choices and portions.

After returning home, it was suggested that guests should have one day per week on a restricted diet. This comprised fruit only in summer and vegetable juices or vegetable soup in winter. A home-based detox week at least twice a year was also recommended.

A research unit with data collection was established with the help of a part-time librarian. The aim was to make available current scientific information relating to nutrition. This was available to the guests, the public, and other interested persons, including Home Economics and Food Science students from the universities.

The topic of colonic irrigation was hotly debated. Eventually, due to various reasons and in common with international practices, the Royal Flush was discontinued. Sister Patience retired home to bake fruit cakes and continued to write poetry.

The original four chiropractors were gradually reduced to one. The previous chiropractors had reached retiring age and the fortunate arrival of Dr Juan van Breda heralded a new method of chiropractic methods. No more 'Crick Crack' but a more gentle body alignment and balancing. Juan van Breda was also knowledgeable about nutrition and medical conditions, thus he was a real asset to the Hydro.

The new lifestyle consultants were all registered nurses who embraced the Hydro philosophy and were keen to implement natural methods and homeopathy instead of pharmaceuticals. On several occasions, serious or previously undiagnosed medical conditions were detected and the guest was speedily referred to the nearby Stellenbosch Hospital or relevant medical specialist. Retired medical doctor, Tim O'Moloney, joined the group and was always available to comfort guests at night or drive them down to hospital if necessary.

On arrival, every guest was allocated to a consultant who prescribed an individual multidisciplinary programme. Blood pressure and weight were measured every second day. Weight loss was always keenly anticipated by the guests who became most upset it the scale did not show favourable results. If the guest had emotional problems, was depressed or grieving, there was a psychologist available for consultations.

Diagnostic blood tests were introduced and a nurse from the pathology services arrived twice weekly to expertly draw blood samples to measure cholesterol, hormones, blood chemistry, and liver and kidney functions, amongst other tests. Male patients tended to be squeamish, so Rescue Remedy was always at hand to calm them down.

The Hydro was still referred to as the 'Fat Farm' by all those who had not experienced its benefits, but slowly perceptions were changing. Clientele included many international visitors who regarded their two weeks at the Hydro as the highlight of their year. Captains of industry, heads of state, politicians and celebrities all merged into uniformity wearing their towelling gowns. Lounging around the pool, one could not detect whether your neighbour was a mining magnate or a fugitive from justice.

To illustrate the feeling of wellbeing, here is an extract from an article written by a 'victim' who had braved a week at the Hydro. "It is the feeling of wellbeing and exhilaration that comes with the return of energy that proves the efficacy of the fast. It is a feeling of having been cleansed and purified. With the detoxifying of the body comes a heightened sense of awareness, increased sensory perception and a reawakening, particularly of the taste buds".

Another former guest wrote: "The transformation from a state of what one thought was normal body functioning to a state of vibrant health and wellbeing was astonishing".

A Swiss guest, Mr L.H., returned home after his stay at the Hydro and wrote: "You advised me to see a heart specialist in Switzerland. He told me that the reason for my being so fit, despite my artery problems, is the treatment I had at the Hydro. The right diet and right exercise kept my heart going".

A well-known politician wrote: "Over the many years that I have been attending the Hydro I have always firmly believed that it is the finest investment I have made in my life".

Mrs E.F. was appreciative of the friendliness of the staff: "My stay was life changing as I have made many resolutions about diet and exercise. The Hydro has always been my personal Shangri-La. The programmes and the peace; the beauty of the scenery; and the solicitous people on the staff".

In 1987, a Stress Management programme was introduced. This was an ambitious undertaking and a forerunner of the many

Corporate Wellness programmes in years to come. It was a seven-day residential programme which aimed to completely rest the individual, and having done so, to educate and introduce coping strategies. Having rested, the participants were far more receptive and were able to absorb information and move towards a stress-coping lifestyle.

The multidisciplinary team included nursing sisters, a nutritionist, chiropractor, masseurs, biokineticians, sports scientists, neuro-physiologists, and communications experts.

The Health Risk Appraisal, using a computerised questionnaire, was a novelty, as was biofeedback, with a visual display showing right or left brain dominance. The majority of business people are left-brain dominant and only a few use the right brain for conceptual and creative thinking.

Right-brain workshops were held by Professor Jaros, head of the Bio-Engineering Department at the University of Cape Town, who introduced novel ways to enhance this underutilised asset in the corporate environment. Other workshops looked at conflict resolution, time management and problem-solving, and were led by communication experts from the University of Cape Town. Daily massage, yoga, breathing exercises, and progressive relaxation were included and the participants did not have time to feel hungry.

At the end of the week or 10 days participants experienced a huge improvement in wellbeing. Blood pressures normalised, digestive problems disappeared, tension in the neck and backache were relieved and insomnia was replaced with peaceful sleep. Persons who had arrived irritable and hostile became calm and friendly.

However, despite its success, employing external facilitators was a costly exercise, and with the programme outcome similar to a normal week's rest with dietary restriction at the Hydro, it was decided to discontinue the Stress Management programme.

It was also during 1987 that the first major upgrading project began. A new amenities wing was built with a heated indoor pool, auditorium, yoga room, skin care clinic, and boutique. General Manager Lawrence Gould organised the grand opening function. The turquoise indoor pool was filled with pink balloons and guests were treated to a lavish salad buffet displaying the Hydro's famous vegetable carvings. Guest speaker was Dr Hannah Reeve Sanders, former Chief Medical Superintendent of Groote Schuur Hospital and Acting Director of Hospital Services, as well as Federal Councillor for the Medical Association. She provided just the right light touch while at the same time adding credibility to the occasion.

Subsequently Dr Nic Lee, editor of the *SA Medical journal* wrote: "The Hydro in Stellenbosch does more for preventive health than any other institution in South Africa".

Following the opening of the new amenities wing, a new men's therapy section was built, followed by the upgrading of the therapy section with 18 massage rooms, and then the women's hydrotherapy area with relaxation rooms. The Hydro was now on a par with any international resort. It was not only South Africa's premier health resort, but it was the first in the country, and in fact one of the first in the world, to integrate Nature Cure with complementary therapies and medical diagnostics. In today's terms it would be regarded as a Medical Spa.

A stay at the Hydro was not expensive by international standards and considering all the inclusive services offered, it was considered a good investment in one's health. In 1972, a week cost R100, which included accommodation, diet, all treatments, daily massage hydrotherapy, and daily chiropractic treatments. In 1990, a similar week cost R2,000.

Accommodation for more than 100 guests was provided in comfortable rooms in the east and west wings, but also more modest and very affordable rooms were available in cottages and mobiles units. During summer months, occupancy reached over 90 per cent, and guests were obliged to book a year in advance so that they could meet their friends in the same place at the same time. 80 per cent of the guests were referred by friends or word of mouth, 50 per cent came from the Western Cape, 25 per cent from Gauteng (or the Transvaal, as it was then called), 5 per cent came from Natal, and 20 per cent were international visitors who often combined a stay at the Hydro with a summer vacation in the Cape.

The majority of guests were female, with 30 per cent males. One amusing side effect of the semi-fasting diet was that the ladies felt amorous whereas the men experienced the opposite effect. With the large preponderance of female guests, single men were very popular.

The University of Cape Town's Department of Biomedical Engineering designed a new device for measuring body composition. Professor Tony Bunn provided the equipment. Known as Bio-Electrical Impedance, it became an accurate tool for measuring body fat. It proved most useful in weight loss programmes and is now utilised globally.

Soon a gymnasium was added, together with exercise classes, and a biokineticist was employed to evaluate problems and recommend suitable exercises for guests. Guests were provided with a printout of their test results together with specifically designed exercises to implement at home. This was valuable for individuals who had previous injuries, hip or knee replacements, back pain, sports injuries, weight problems, as well as the elderly. The Hydro was the first resort in South Africa to introduce water aerobics, or Aquacise, which proved to be very popular as well as therapeutic.

The Hydrotherapy department was enlarged to incorporate Kneipp therapy, a first in South Africa. This water treatment was originally devised in Germany by Father Sebastian Kneipp who cured himself of ill health by applications of cold water bathing, alternating with warm water. Bad Worishofen, home of the Kneipp School, taught the method of alternating water temperatures, and also the principles of diet and exercise. Guests at the Hydro regarded the Sitz bath – a bath in which a person sat up to the hips in water which alternated between warm and icy cold – as a form of torture, as they did the hosing-down with jets of cold water. Foot baths and arm baths were tolerable and these were effective in improving circulation and stimulating the immune system. Guests were encouraged to have a cold shower every day on returning home and to apply skin brushing.

Another first in South Africa was Thalassotherapy, the medical use of seaweed and sea water as a form of therapy. Quiberon in France, was a major centre for this excellent and very effective treatment. In South Africa, along the coast of the Western Cape, were vast beds of Ecklonia Maxima, or Kelp, as it is commonly known. This brown seaweed is a rich source of vitamins and minerals as well as oligosaccharides, which have excellent moisturising properties. Thus seaweed treatments with Ecklonia Maxima were introduced at the Hydro in 1992 and proved to be very popular. The seaweed wraps and baths stimulated metabolism and enhanced weight loss.

Not all the new treatments were a success, however. In the late 1980s, flotation tanks, a form of 'restricted environmental stimulation therapy' or REST, were introduced. The idea was to enter a cylinder shaped rather like a large coffin, and float in luke-warm water which had a high concentration of salt. One floated in darkness in total silence. This was supposed to create calm and reduce stress. The Hydro installed two flotation tanks and invited feedback from guests. The outcome was quite the opposite to that which had been documented in other current literature. Some guests became panicky and others claustrophobic. Blood pressures rose instead of dropping. The flotation tanks were removed.

Successful therapies introduced included Reiki, Shiatsu and Reflexology – all at a time when they were new in South Africa. Lily Daschner, who trained in the Vodder School of manual lymphatic drainage, arrived from Europe. Introduced at the Hydro, this was also a first in South Africa. Lymphatic drainage was an effective treatment in management of fluid retention, cellulite, lymphedema and other health problems.

Of course, chiropractic treatment continued to be an important part of each guest's return to health and Juan van Breda was able to relieve many back and neuromuscular problems.

Gradually the stigma of 'freakiness' was broken down. Medical doctors were invited to functions and the Medical Association

Branch Council enjoyed a special day in the glorious surroundings. Nutrition students from the University of Cape Town and dieticians from Stellenbosch University were impressed with the superb buffets and displays of salads. Visiting international celebrities in nutritional medicine and complementary therapies were invited to lecture guests in the auditorium.

In 1993, Dr Fred Sanders, editor of the *Journal of Continuing Medical Education*, a publication circulated to all registered medical practitioners, reported on his week spent at the Hydro. His conclusion was that each person needed to assume responsibility for his/her own health and work at maintaining it, rather than seeking help to cure disease. "Places like High Rustenburg Hydro provide a necessary jump start for a healthier lifestyle".

This was echoed by one of the regular guests. Chief M.B. wrote in 1999: "I live every day in the hope that we will come again to the Hydro. I have always looked forward to your wonderful care whenever we were your patients. We were great admirers of Mr Saporetti when he was alive. Generations to come need to know what he did for humanity in establishing the Hydro for all of us".

Cleto Saporetti bequeathed his fortune to "the people of South Africa". His vision was to improve the health of all South Africans by promoting a healthy lifestyle with the emphasis on optimal nutrition.

There was no other health resort in the country – and perhaps very few, if any, internationally – where community outreach projects, nutrition education for the underprivileged, together with research involving universities and tertiary facilities, were integrated into the day-to-day activities of the resort.

Chiropractic, acupuncture, reflexology, aromatherapy and homeopathy were later accepted and registered with the Allied Health Professions Council of South Africa. During the nineties, many student interns came to the Hydro in order to learn about nutrition and lifestyle modification. Recently, Naturopathy courses were introduced at the University of the Western Cape. Cleto Saporetti was ahead of his time.

What contributed to the success of the Hydro? It had a soul, it had a heart. This was quite palpable. All guests felt part of the Hydro family. They were welcomed as friends on arrival and watched over by the benign presence of Cleto Saporetti, whose portrait hung in reception.

THE CLETO SAPORETTI FOUNDATION
1986–2002

*The health of the people is really
the foundation upon which all the
power of the nation depends.*
(Disraeli)

There were very clear instructions regarding the Foundation in Saporetti's will.

"The object of the Foundation shall be:
- research into and the study of Nature Cure/Naturopathy with diet being of great importance;
- teaching and practice of Nature Cure/Naturopathy;
- propagation and spreading of the philosophy and practice of Nature Cure."

Saporetti went on to state: "I believe that these objectives will be in the interest of the peoples of South Africa leading to higher standards of health and wellbeing".

He further specified how the available funds were to be utilised:

- Funds should be allocated to establish a chair of Naturopathy at a university; OR to the establishment of a research unit which would spread knowledge relating to Naturopathy;
- Clinics to be established which would promote the practice of Naturopathy and provide assistance to underprivileged persons;
- Establishment of a Senior Citizens' home.

When Geraldine Mitton was appointed as Director of the Cleto Saporetti Foundation, and also Medical Director of the Hydro, the duties drawn up by Graeme Dale Kuys, the curator of Saporetti's estate, were in keeping with Cleto's wishes. Dale Kuys and Cleto had spent many hours discussing ways in which the work of the Foundation could be recognised and accepted by the Medical and Dental Council, as well as government authorities, universities, and other tertiary organisations.

Thus Dr Mitton's duties were to:

- head the therapeutic staff at the Hydro and continue to implement the practice of Naturopathy;
- research the benefits of naturopathy/holistic/complementary/ integrated medicine and disseminate information to the South African public;
- establish contact with the South African Medical and Dental Council and Medical Association of South Africa to encourage acceptance of the Hydro philosophy as a means to attaining optimum health;

- encourage and maintain co-operation with universities and tertiary organisations;
- establish Senior Citizens' home and other clinics.

In the previous chapter we saw how Saporetti's wishes were implemented successfully at the Hydro, which obtained credibility within the medical profession, as well as gained the confidence of the public.

The objects of the Foundation were implemented in tandem with the Hydro but the challenge was to take the message out into the community.

The area adjacent to the Hydro was Ida's Valley, a township which was home to many less privileged people. Nearby was another township, Cloetesville. In these townships there was a problem of gangsterism and alcohol abuse. It was decided that, instead of spending a huge sum of money on establishing a Chair of Naturopathy at the University, which was not yet acceptable in 1986, or even a Chair of Nutrition, a great deal more could be achieved by 'grass roots' nutrition and health education.

The Stellenbosch district covers an area of about 850 square kilometres and the idea was to appoint 'nutrition educators' who would go out into the community to assess needs and implement programmes. It was important to choose educators who came from the community themselves, who were accepted by the people, and who were knowledgeable about conditions in the district.

Geraldine Mitton was fortunate to have Cornelia Kirsten as a co-worker. Cornelia was a registered dietician, had a teaching degree, and her computer skills made data collection and gathering of statistics for research projects that much easier.

During the first few years, considerable time was spent in meeting health professionals throughout South Africa. Many talks and lectures were given to the public at conferences, both in South Africa and internationally, and also on radio and television. Research projects were planned with Stellenbosch University and the University of Cape Town. Talks were given at women's groups and high profile functions. These were very popular because the Hydro offered sought-after prizes of a day or a week at the Hydro. General Manager Lawrence Gould saw the benefit of public profile development and was enthusiastic in promoting the Hydro philosophy as well as the Foundation.

Nutrition Education

During 1987, the Stellenbosch Divisional Council gave permission to the Saporetti Foundation to sponsor Nutrition Educators. They accepted that the aim was to reach a large population group and to educate them in correct and cost-effective dietary practices. Instead of focussing on the establishment of a single clinic, the alternative was to take nutrition and health promotion to the many communities in the Stellenbosch district. The first two ladies were chosen from Ida's Valley and began their training with the House of Representatives, taking part in field work as well as lectures. Examined at monthly intervals, they received a Diploma in Nutrition Education after one year. The number of nutrition educators was increased to six, and the Hydro supplied two vehicles which enabled them to visit the farms, clinics, crèches and schools in the Stellenbosch district. The Cleto Saporetti Mobile Nutrition Unit became a regular sight amongst the Stellenbosch community. Local farmers often called to request assistance on their farms.

The educators gave cooking demonstrations, lectures and very popular role play sessions at clinics, schools, crèches and on farms where they identified malnourished children and referred them for proper attention. They organised baby competitions, set up rummage sales to raise funds, and developed housewives' clubs to help counteract alcohol abuse.

In poor communities the purchase of expensive meat meant that there were very small portions to provide for large families, and it was usually the man and father who took the major share. During nutrition demonstrations the educators showed how beans or lentils as alternative protein sources could be incorporated into family meals.

Senior citizens

Instead of building a single old age home it was decided to target several homes and groups in the Stellenbosch district. In this way, a much larger target audience could be reached. The nutrition educators formed a pensioners' group in Macassar and held annual Senior Citizens' Fun days.

Visiting the Mfuleni old age home in Cloetesville they gave foot baths and massages to painful feet. At the official opening of the Mfuleni Community Centre on April 28th, 1990, special tribute was paid to the outstanding help from the Saporetti Foundation.

A Geriatrics sports day, held at the University of the Western Cape, hosted 53 teams from throughout the Western Cape. The team led by the Saporetti Foundation's nutrition educators were overall winners.

During the Geriatric week, which was held in Ida's Valley and Cloetesville, the Saporetti team built a float to join the parade on September 15th, 1990. Sporting baskets of fruit and vegetables, their theme was "You are what you eat".

As time went on, more senior citizens were targeted and the Simonsberg Christian Centre was the venue for a fancy dress occasion with the rejuvenated residents wearing outfits resembling vegetables.

The Catholic Noah Home, close to the Hydro, also received attention and donations. The annual Senior Citizens' Day, first implemented by the nutrition educators, was adopted by the municipality who held similar programmes at the town hall for up to 500 seniors. At the other end of the spectrum, a 'Mr Muscles' competition was held for pre-school children at Lourensford Estate in Somerset West.

Research projects

Meanwhile students from the Department of Community Health at the University of Cape Town attended lectures at the Hydro about the work of the Foundation and subsequently undertook research projects evaluating risk factor measurement at the Hydro.

Combined projects with the Rural Foundation and with USKOR (University Stellenbosch Klinieke Organasie) were undertaken. One of the senior lecturers from USKOR spent a week at the Hydro and wrote: "I would like to convey a personal word of gratitude for the opportunity I had of making such a worthwhile investment in my health and wellbeing. I can assure you that through the holistic approach, I was restored form the brink of total breakdown to a sense of balance, perspective, health and physical energy which I did not think possible".

A group of medical doctors from the Department of Family Medicine, Stellenbosch University, visited the Hydro for a Health Day of lectures and, of course, the famous salad buffet. One could always be certain of a good attendance by the medical profession who enjoyed the beautiful environment and the novelty of the Hydro's approach to health.

Dr A.J.B., from the Medical Research Council National Region of Nutritional Intervention, wrote in 1992: "We have a better knowledge of the excellent work you are doing. I think that we have all recognised the unique opportunity of collaboration that exists between our organisations. We are looking forward to collaborating with you in the field of nutrition".

Cleto Saporetti would have been very happy to hear of this!

Biofeedback research was undertaken by the Department of Biomedical Engineering at UCT. A Masters student created a device measuring right and left brain functions which could be used for stress management. Statistics obtained from the participants of the Stress Management programmes held during 1987 and 1988 revealed some interesting findings: 48 per cent of the participants suffered from tension headaches; 50 per cent had backache, neck and shoulder tension; 56 per cent had indigestion; 48 per cent consumed excess caffeine; 36 per cent consumed more than two units of alcohol daily;

27 per cent were smokers; 63 per cent were below average physical fitness; 78 per cent had elevated cholesterol levels; 18 per cent had high blood pressure; and 43 per cent regularly missed breakfast. As previously mentioned, after a week of rest and relaxation, together with a restricted diet, there was a significant improvement in well-being as well as the motivation to change to a healthy lifestyle.

The Foundation offices at the Hydro collected data and established a library covering many aspects of preventive health, weight control, physical fitness, nutrition, relaxation techniques, complementary therapies, stress management, women's health and men's health. This information was available to guests, students, university personnel, and to the public.

Stellenbosch University students from the Department of Home Economics conducted research projects and their head, Professor Leonie Van Heerden, organised the first Vegetable Gardens Com-petition for the Stellenbosch community.

Continuing education for staff at the Hydro

One realised that the therapy staff, including masseurs, needed to be kept abreast of current knowledge of health and wellness. Many of them did not have prior training in anatomy. Thus a weekly lecture series was implemented by some of the nurses leading to a year-long, in-house Diploma in Wellness.

Vegetable Gardens Competition

This was a major success and credit must be given to Leonie van Heerden, who drew up the entry forms which were then distributed to the Divisional Council clinics. The first competition was held in 1986 and there were 120 entries. Many applicants had never grown vegetables before. Generous prizes were awarded to the group and to individuals who were able to create the most attractive vegetable gardens. Judging was done by Professor van Heerden, Ron Hobkirk, Cornelia Kirsten and university students. The winner received a colour television set, with a stove and a fridge going to second and third prize winners.

These competitions continued annually until 1999, with increasing numbers of entries. By 1999, there were 500 entries which proved to be a headache for the judges. Apart from the large number of vegetable gardens to be judged, the area covered was considerable and the Foundation mobile units had to travel far and wide. Each year different sectors were identified. One year was devoted to farm workers, another to township dwellers, and a heart-warming effort was realised in 1994 when informal settlements were targeted. 'Smarty Town' shack dwellers managed to devote every piece of outdoor space to growing vegetables.

The township dwellers were shown how to grow sufficient vegetables, on a door-sized plot, to feed a family of five. Seeds were obtained from Food Gardens Unlimited. It was encouraging to see how families benefited from eating fresh vegetables. An unexpected benefit was that alcohol consumption decreased in men who were now involved in competing for worthwhile prizes. Children helped with the weeding and grannies assisted with watering.

Stellenbosch University students, including 40 third year students with their senior lecturer, conducted a research project involving 20 families living on two farms. The aim was to improve family health by vegetable gardening and to give the students practice and experience in community development through vegetable gardening.

Problems encountered included pests and pets. Families required continuous encouragement. There were social problems within families.

50 per cent of the subjects were first-time gardeners and there was a 20 per cent dropout rate. The students noted that alcohol intake dropped, and dagga consumption and smoking markedly decreased. Each family was adopted by two students who had the theoretical knowledge of the new method. The Saporetti nutrition educators acted as mediators between students and families and the participants were motivated because they were entered into the annual vegetable garden competition.

The Schools' Health Fair

This was a first in South Africa. A major undertaking, its success was due to the ongoing contact by the Foundation staff who visited local schools in Ida's Valley and Cloetesville. The idea was that each school should choose a project from a list of health topics incorporating the various aspects of a healthy lifestyle. The purpose of the Health Fair was to provide health information in a simple way; to promote healthy food choices, exercise and fitness; and to prevent unhealthy lifestyle habits such as smoking, alcohol and drug abuse. Each school designed a stand with posters and models, and pupils would then talk and demonstrate the principles involved. Some of the projects included: "Have a healthy Heart"; "Stop Smoking"; "Health and Hygiene go Hand in Hand"; "Growing Vegetables; "Care of your

Teeth"; and "Don't do Drugs". First prize went to the primary school whose pupils portrayed "Health and Hygiene go Hand in Hand".

The nutrition educators visited the schools weekly to see how they were progressing. The Health Fair was held on the last two days of term in March 1993. Over 6,000 children formed queues and marched from their schools to the main hall of Cloetesville High. Excitement, anticipation, and pride in their achievements were reflected in their happy faces. The SA Police and Traffic Department officials supplied a friendly presence with emphasis on the importance of traffic rules and good road sense. The National Cancer Association took the opportunity to make the children aware of the pitfalls of an unhealthy lifestyle.

After the opening function, the Mayor and Mayoress of Stellenbosch, the Inspector of Schools and various dominees spoke on behalf of the community, noting that the project had created a unifying effect. It had proved to be a partial deterrent to the emerging problem of drugs and gangsterism.

The Saporetti Community Centre

At last an ideal house for this project was found in the township of Cloetesville. It belonged to the Stellenbosch Municipality who had agreed to allow its use by the Saporetti Foundation. There was only one problem; the house had been appropriated by squatters. They were not just ordinary squatters, but Rastafarians allegedly dealing in dagga. After some persuasion they agreed to leave and the next step was to repair and paint the building including both exterior and interior rooms. University students came forward with great energy, applying their creative talents to murals, bright colours, and a Jungle Gym. A vegetable garden was created outside. Offices were established for counselling, and programmes for children were implemented. A pre-school group in the morning gave children a meal while they were taught basic hygiene and manners. After school, other children were entertained instead of playing in the streets and being exposed to drug peddlers. A number of housewives were happy to become involved and volunteered their services in return for education and assistance with their children. Children were fed each day with vegetables obtained from the Hydro, together with the famous Hydro health bread.

The Healthy Valley Concept

This concept was drawn up to provide a comprehensive community-based health programme for the inhabitants of Ida's Valley township. It was only partly realised due to lack of funding. An attempt was made to attract external funding, but this was not successful because other organisations saw the Hydro and its connected Saporetti Foundation as not being in need of financial support.

During 1991, Dr Derek Browne, a general practitioner from the UK, visited the Hydro to look at the Foundation's community projects. He had previously met Mitton at an international health conference in Helsinki. Using the model of the Healthy Valley, he developed a similar 'Healthy Village' concept in the UK with more success after he started giving talks, writing papers, and lobbying the British government. At his presentations, including the 1999 World

Health Organisation meeting in Malaysia, he always mentioned the South African Healthy Valley model as his inspiration.

The British government allocated £300 million for the Healthy Village project to be implemented in the year 2000.

It was a sad day when, in 2002, the activities of the Foundation ceased, with the sale of the Hydro in the same year, and the closing down of the Community Health Centre. Saporetti's intention was that the Foundation would exist 'in perpetuity'. However, this was not to be. It was essentially connected to the Hydro and when the latter was sold the Foundation could not continue unaided. There are several reasons why the trustees decided to sell the Hydro and it is not the purpose of this book to discuss them. The last remaining project was the Community Centre in the township of Cloetesville. The centre offered activities and support to preschool children. It reverted to the municipality and was subsequently demolished.

The Saporetti Foundation came into being, expanded and developed over a period of 16 years. Despite its discontinuation, its influence continued in the many initiatives implemented during the years of its activities, and this continues in the Stellenbosch communities today.

LEGACY

What you leave behind is not
what is engraved on monuments
but what is woven into
the lives of others.
(Pericles)

It is an achievement that High Rustenburg Hydro still exists four decades after its humble beginnings in 1972. From the initial three rooms it grew to accommodate a hundred guests and provided world class facilities and services.

The Hydro has relaxed the stringent "one fruit three times a day" regime of controlled fasting. It now offers guests larger portions and a choice of salads and cooked vegetables. Guests can choose to detox on a restricted diet, or enjoy *a la carte* vegetarian cuisine. Coffee is still taboo and fresh vegetable juices and herbal teas are acceptable alternatives.

As the first health resort in South Africa to integrate complementary therapies with medical diagnostics, evolving from the original Nature Cure, yet maintaining its original philosophy, the Hydro was ahead of its time.

It is remarkable that Saporetti had this vision in 1970. He was tireless in his efforts to gain acceptance by the medical fraternity. With determination and disregard for obstacles and other people's criticisms, he carried out his plans. He had the belief, commitment and courage to pursue his dreams.

Even more remarkable is that he made provision in his will for the establishment of the Cleto Saporetti Foundation and that both facilities and activities should be integrated. This was a first in South Africa and probably the first internationally.

If only his Italian dream had been realised, there would have been a second Hydro and Saporetti Foundation established in Italy, close to his home town of Ravenna. In a country of many spas and hydrothermal resorts, with a culture of robust Italian cuisine, Saporetti's Hydro would have been unique.

However, the Hydro is first and foremost a present and hopefully lasting testament to his vision. Many thousands of guests have passed through its doors and have absorbed and practised the principles of a healthy lifestyle with the emphasis on nutrition and diet.

The Hydro was a pioneer, introducing new therapies into South Africa. Water aerobics, Kneipp hydrotherapy, manual lymphatic drainage, and Thalassotherapy all had their beginnings in Stellenbosch. Equipment for measuring body fat was first evaluated at the Hydro and is now utilised globally. The stress management programmes were forerunners of today's many and varied Corporate Wellness workshops. It is a matter for speculation that one of the factors contributing to the inclusion of complementary therapies into registration with the Allied Health Professions Board of South

Africa, was the grassroots initiatives introduced in the Hydro forty years ago.

One of the former nutrition educators, Ansaaf Crombie, rose through the ranks in the Stellenbosch Municipality. She says that her training and qualification as Nutrition Advisor with the Department of Health was an asset in her promotion. She is now a town councillor, continuing with community development projects in the Stellenbosch district and utilises the knowledge and experience gained through her years with the Foundation.

Geraldine Mitton published her book, *The Anti-aging Handbook*, which incorporates all the knowledge acquired during her 14 years at the Hydro. Dedicated to Cleto Saporetti, it offers the A to Z guidelines of healthy living, integrating both orthodox and complementary therapies. This book has resulted in invitations to speak at many conferences internationally, from South East Asia to Europe and the US.

She has had the opportunity to assist the American organisers of the Global Spa Summit from 2008 to 2010. Based in New York, the Global Spa Summit meets in a different country each year and attracts leaders in the hospitality, health, and spa industries who debate current and future trends in their respective countries. In 2008, keynote speaker Dr Richard Carmona, former US Surgeon General, spoke about the vital role that health resorts had in promoting health. "Instead of a Health-Care system, we have a Sick-Care system," he said. "We have a disease burden that is largely preventible. In the spa industry we have the opportunity to move people on to the path of optimal health and wellness."

At subsequent international summits in 2009 and 2010, Geraldine Mitton was able to lead workshops to encourage health resorts to incorporate preventive health into spas. Over 60 per cent of delegates voted to introduce health promoting initiatives in their spas. It was decided that research validating the health benefits of spa therapies would be valuable. As a result the website, *Spaevidence.com* was established. This site allows research into the benefits of massage, hydrotherapy, reflexology, yoga and many other complementary therapies according to evidence-based research projects conducted by leading academic institutions.

In 2010, Mitton was invited by the Department of Health Tourism in the Philippines to discuss how medical clinics and hospitals could combine with spas to promote preventive health, recuperation, and rehabilitation. This was one of the aims of the Hydro, together with initiatives to partner with medical aid societies. The Philippines is one of several countries internationally which are now promoting Health Tourism.

It has been a long battle to create changes in attitude by medical schools and government bodies but the world has gradually awakened to the need for preventive health measures.

A combined report from a group of sports medicine doctors from the US, UK, Switzerland, Canada, Holland, Sweden Norway and South Africa was published in 2011. It stated: "The disparity between our scientific knowledge about chronic disease and practical implementation of preventive approaches is one of the most urgent concerns in healthcare worldwide and threatens the collapse of our health systems unless extraordinary change takes place".

The doctors noted that medical schools currently focus on disease-based healthcare and this is compounded by drug companies who encourage constant medication. It would appear that conventional medicine and wellness are in competition. These doctors have submitted their report to medical schools in their respective countries, hoping to stimulate change. They have also recommended the inclusion of 'Holism' which would make use of complementary therapies in the management of chronic illnesses.

The Hydro was a centre where guests were educated to take individual responsibility for their health. They then had the power to remain healthy through lifestyle choices. The Saporetti Foundation implemented many initiatives to collaborate with the medical world, universities and government bodies. Numerous public talks, media coverage, radio and television appearances focussed on the benefits of lifestyle changes, while also promoting complementary therapies. In one memorable television debate, Mitton went head-to-head with a well-known professor of Medicine who declared that "Aromatherapy is a load of rubbish and has no effect because the oils cannot be absorbed through the skin". The year was 1989. Today there are many transdermal preparations which are effectively applied as creams, oils or patches.

The legacy lives on

The community work in Stellenbosch, led by Ansaaf Crombie as town councillor, continues to experience the positive effects of Cleto's legacy.

In 1986 vegetable gardens were a novelty; it was a great achievement that by 1999 there were 500 entries in the annual competition. Many of these first-time gardeners have continued to provide a valuable source of nutrition for their families.

The Senior Citizens' Health Days, started by the Foundation, have now become an annual event, organised by government bodies. Many of the old age homes in the Stellenbosch district have continued with the events started by the Foundation.

Hundreds of women educated in healthy nutrition at clinics have continued to use the knowledge for the benefit of their families.

The 6,000 school children who took part in the Health Fair are citizens of the future. The knowledge gained at this huge event, covering so many aspects of healthy living, will remain with them in years to come. Apart from the health education aspect, this event resulted in cohesion and co-operation between municipal bodies and the Education Department.

The Healthy Valley project spread its roots to England where the Healthy Village concept was created on the same principles. In Stellenbosch, the inhabitants of Ida's valley have been encouraged and enabled to adopt the principles of healthy living.

Born of a dream

From leaving Zonderwater Prison with just a few pounds in his pocket, to realising his vision of health promotion for all the people of South Africa, Cleto Saporetti faced challenges that would have destroyed most men. He was universally respected and admired, not only for his business acumen and entrepreneurship, but for his generosity and philanthropy. He leaves behind a legacy that continues to benefit hundreds of thousands of people.

All those who have contributed memories and anecdotes to this book have only the most special memories of his friendship.

ABOUT THE AUTHOR

Geraldine Mitton is a pioneer in integrated medicine and preventive health, combining her scientific knowledge with complementary therapies and naturopathy.

She was Medical Director of The High Rustenburg Hydro and the Cleto Saporetti Foundation from 1986–2002. Prior to this position, she was the Head of Emergency Unit, Groote Schuur Hospital, Cape Town, where she was involved in the management of many lifestyle-related illnesses.

She has consulted in the development of medical and destination spas in South Africa and countries in the rest of the world, mainly in South East Asia. Her *Anti-ageing Handbook* is available internationally.

Dr Mitton has also created and implemented community outreach programmes focusing on health promotion and nutrition education for the less privileged in South Africa.